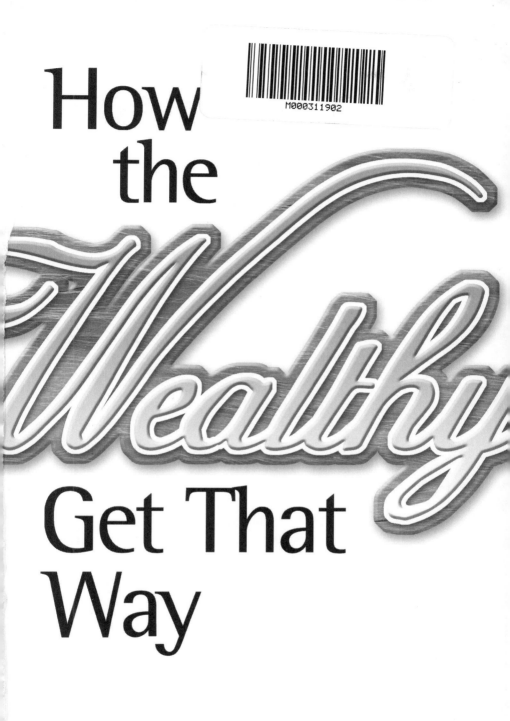

How the
the
Wealthy
Get That
Way

The first
million's
the hardest!

How the *Wealthy* Get That Way

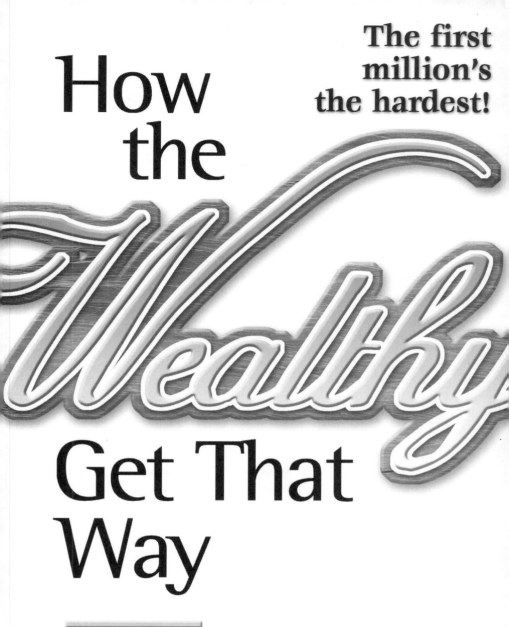

Dr. Edward L. Silker
Dr. Herman and Diana Boehme

Silk Pages Publishing • Deerwood, Minnesota

Publisher:
Silk Pages Publishing
21343 Archibald Road
Deerwood, Minnesota 56444
1-800-450-0091

Library of Congress Control Number: 2002091873

ISBN: 0-9645815-2-3

Dedication

This book is dedicated to all those aspiring souls
who are willing to put forth the effort
to attain financial freedom.

TABLE OF CONTENTS

DISCLAIMER

This publication contains the ideas, opinions, and findings of its authors. It is sold with the understanding that the authors and publisher are not engaged in rendering legal, accounting, investment or other professional services. Laws vary from state to state and federal laws must be taken into consideration. If the reader requires expert financial, legal, or other advice, a competent professional should be consulted. Neither the authors nor the publisher can guarantee the accuracy of the information contained herein.

The authors and publisher specifically disclaim any responsibility for any liability, loss, or risk, personal or otherwise, which is incurred as a consequence, directly or indirectly, of the use and application of any of the contents of this book.

INTRODUCTION

"Nothing will come of nothing"
Shakespeare

HOW DO THE WEALTHY get that way? That is the direction of this fascinating journey we are about to embark on.

No, we are not writing about some genius who reinvented the world in his dad's garage. This is about you obtaining financial independence and living a very successful life. We do not measure success by outward symbols; how big a boat you own, or where your home is located.

Wealth is when you are happy, healthy and can sleep at night without having to worry about how you are going to pay the bills. It is not when you have an enormous amount of money, but when you are in a financial position where you no longer have to expend your precious time and energy on monetary concerns.

This book is dedicated to helping you find yourself and to obtaining the wealth that is within everyone's reach. By accepting full responsibility for your past and current circumstances, both financial and otherwise, you will be in a much more favorable position to attain your dreams. It is too easy to blame someone else for ones misfortune, and live in a constant mindset of, "If I only had a rich relative, or if only the stock I picked had gone up." It is *you* that makes all your decisions, good or bad. These apparent failures can much more constructively be viewed as "stepping stones to success" and thus become useful lessons which help direct us to our ultimate goals. By accepting the postulate that "there are no accidents," one significantly enhances one's likelihood of a bright future.

Herein lies a very critical point. It's not what happens to us, but how we react to what happens to us which determines our destiny. This is regularly being demonstrated in our daily environment. The very same challenge presents to two individuals. This challenge drives one person to destruction and motivates the other to not only rise to the challenge, but stimulates him on to extreme heights of success. Careful observation will reveal many examples where the very same stimulus results in drastically different results. The cause of the divergent results is directly related to the way the individuals mentally process the stimulus.

One may view a travel delay as extremely frustrating while another looks on with favor and an internal knowing that the delay is in their best interest. The one who has arrived at a mental state where "everything always works out for his best interest" has obviously evolved to an extremely advantageous position for everything to go his way.

Once we fully accept that we are completely in control of our destiny, our life journey becomes a special and exciting adventure. Today's decisions and actions are exactly what determine our future station in life. A high school dropout will have very limited opportunities compared to those who complete their education. As more education is attained, more doors of opportunity open.

We would be amiss to suggest that this is so easy that everyone can achieve every desired goal without paying the price. Success often requires a complete change of the current mindset. For instance, as a baby, *no* is a word heard repeatedly. So is it any wonder that young adults often attempt to dismiss it? For example, the 'no' to an extra can of beer, the 'no' to drugs and to other things that their better judgment tells them is wrong. The tendency to dismiss the 'no' coupled with constant peer pressure at times result in individuals setting in motion causes which are in the long run negative in nature. This is not unique to the young, but is the pitfall for many adults as well. For instance, credit is often very easily obtained and the outstanding balance created can be so very hard to pay back. This is why many people find themselves desperately trapped in the proverbial financial merry-go-round, because they can not break the habit of impulse buying. Credit cards, which the astute marketing experts make so convenient, are wonderful if you pay them off each month without accruing interest; otherwise you start digging a big financial hole for yourself and make the credit card company rich as you pay incredible amounts of accumulating interest.

It always saddens me when I see hard-working, well-educated people nearing retirement age and finding themselves financially ill-prepared for what could have been pleasant years ahead. Why does this happen to so many? It is mostly a lack of planning and procrastination about starting an investment/savings plan during their working years.

In this book, we endeavor to stimulate your thinking and equip you with tools which will help prevent such an occurrence from happening to you, and afford you opportunity to provide financial freedom throughout your life.

We all know that early planning is an important key to financial success. With this common knowledge so prevalent, why don't more people begin early? The answer to that question is that we, as a group, often tend to procrastinate about committing to a regular savings program. Also we become trapped in the overconsumption mode where we succumb to the 'enjoy now, pay later' marketing campaigns which have us scrambling just to make monthly payments, leaving us no extra cash with which to invest.

Our intention in this dissertation is to show interested and disciplined individuals a way in which they can either avoid this trap if they discover this book soon enough, or work their way out of their financial dilemma if they are in one. Armed with the information herein provided, it is possible to learn early on: the benefit of a personal budget, the impact of the interest factor, the value in acquiring assets which appreciate, the need to set up a systematic savings plan, study the opportunities of investment in the dynamic securities of the great corporations of our nation and much more which will aid the astute in their financial journey. These efforts, when applied with discipline and consistency, will ensure your financial success both during the working years and after retirement.

By the time we have completed this journey together, you will know how to become financially independent, and the ball will be in your court. If you put these principles to work and stick with them, financial success is virtually assured. The decision is entirely yours.

After you finish the last chapter and put the book down, you will realize you are in control of your financial destiny. Here is hoping you enjoy your journey through the pages as much as we enjoyed preparing them for you, and that we have piqued your interest enough that you will decide to take the high road and start a serious savings campaign no later than today.

Happy savings and investing, and may the financial rewards for your efforts overwhelm you. You are a very special person and you deserve it.

THE DRIVING
FORCE

THAT BURNING DESIRE

"There is no greatness without a passion to be great, whether it's the aspiration of an athlete or an artist, a scientist, a parent, or a businessman."
Anthony Robbins, Unlimited Power

THAT BURNING DESIRE, more powerful than all other factors, is present in the vast majority of the success stories studied. It is described by various people whom we might describe as financially independent as "all consuming," "inherent," "innate," "intuitive," "overwhelming," "vivid," "uncontrollable," and "dominating all other thoughts."

But as you might ask, where does this burning desire come from, and how can I get one? Well, it seems there is no one source and therefore there are many ways to induce or stimulate your desire to get it burning ferociously. Some, like myself, report the burning desire from a very early age, while others cultivate it well into adulthood. It can be a desire to escape poverty or it can be a yearning to attain a level reached by someone highly respected or perhaps of some other etiology totally unrelated to either of these issues. It can come when one is engrossed in deep thought on the subject or when in a leisurely mode far removed from serious thought.

Also be aware when it does come, it can ignite explosively like a rampant out of control forest fire or it can just be a subtle thought which is capable of smoldering for years like an old peat bog fire in the middle of a forest and never be anything more than a smoldering mass. So just as the first flicker from the campfire requires constant fanning and nurturing to survive, so might some of our thoughts need constant stimulation to grow into burning desires. "But how can I stimulate that initial spark?" you ask. First let's analyze what is that initial spark. Upon careful examination it seems to be a thought backed by emotion. Are these (thought and emotion) equal, nearly equal, or far from equal? Much study on the subject has led to the conclusion they are far from equal. Thoughts are things, and very powerful things. All great and worthwhile accomplishments had their beginnings with the initial thought at the moment of its conception. For it is obvious no one can accomplish physically anything which has not first been perceived as a thought. Therefore without the thought, the accomplishment can never become a reality.

Now that we understand the extreme role thought plays in the burning desire phenomenon which motivates great people to success, we must reveal that the emotional component totally dwarfs the important thought factor. By the magnitude of all the beaches in the world to a single grain of sand, emotion stands over thought, for though thought is necessary, only strong emotion has the power to carry on through all the obstacles, frustrations, apparent defeats, disappointments, struggles, sacrifices, and dead ends which are inherent in accomplishing worthwhile goals.

So in the final analysis, emotion is tantamount to burning desire. Only those worthwhile thoughts which are completely impregnated with emotion to the extent their possessor takes a stance which says "I will accomplish this feat or die trying" are assured of being brought to fruition. Only the power of strong emotion has the energy to keep on keeping on when everyone around you and at times even your inner self is shouting against such action.

Now that we know the importance of the emotion behind our thoughts, what can we do to kindle that spark of emotion into a rampaging inferno? WOW! Just the thought of this gets the blood rushing. When you can feel your heart rate accelerate, your blood pressure rise, and an intense fluttering sensation in your gut that propels you into an orbit which feels far above planet Earth, you are experiencing the sensation which powers great achievement. The key is to find a thought which stimulates your emotional trigger strongly enough to put you into this euphoric state. Let your imagination run wild as to what your goal in life might be; when the motivating goal is discovered you will experience feelings similar to those above. Then dwell on the thought of your goal and your emotional fortitude will provide the necessary energy to accomplish your goal. *How the Wealthy Get That Way* will provide some interesting insights into how you might proceed on your own unique and exciting journey.

As Rudolph Flesch put it in his *The Art of Readable Writing*, "When the mind is busy with something else, or when we are relaxing or asleep, anything goes. Our unconscious just keeps toying with idea combinations regardless of whether they make sense or not."

And then — 'out of nowhere' — comes the flash of inspiration.

The goal of this dissertation is to provide information which may be of value to those who are so inclined, have the mental discipline, and the internal fortitude necessary to achieve the state of financial freedom commonly referred to as "independent wealth." This term is admittedly quite subjective and will by definition vary considerably among evaluators. Only the individual herself can place a number on it which is personally appropriate. While many who take this rhetoric journey may be thrilled attaining the "millionaire" status, others may have already attained that goal or be nearing it and choose to set their sights higher. Some may be quite content with a few hundred thousand dollars as their ultimate net worth. The actual goal of our fellow travelers on this voyage is individual and a matter for each person to feel comfortable with within their own mental framework.

The adventure will be one of discovering what techniques, strategies, planning, and foresight have proven successful for those who have already reached their goals. This path we are about to travel together leads toward wealth. It is up to you to pursue it to the degree and magnitude which is comfortable and beneficial in your unique set of circumstances which comprise your life. Your ultimate success, which will be determined by a law far greater than any laws set forth by man, will be commensurate with the effort you put forth.

The rules are the same for all, for those who have succeeded previously, all currently on the path, and all who will follow in the near or distant future. These rules, findings, discoveries, or whatever you choose to name them are universal, unchanging, consistent, and always in effect, just as are all the other laws of nature such as gravity, momentum, nuclear orbits, valences, and vacuum. All the above are consistent and work equally well for any one individual as for all others. Therefore if Amanda or Zachary jump off the dock, they both fall down into the water in compliance with the law of gravity and if either or both comply with similar laws of prosperity they will succeed to the degree they expend their energies there. These laws are not only consistent, they are inescapable and will always apply.

The path we are taking looks at some of the fundamentals the "independently wealthy" ahead of us have found on their journeys. From the wonderful book *The Millionaire Next Door* by Stanley and Danko, (a must read), we learn they divide the millionaires into two subsets. One subset being first generation wealthy who have come from varied but not wealthy families. The second subset being second, third, fourth, or more generation wealthy. From this latter group we learn little. If we were not born into wealth, which this discussion presupposes, we can hardly follow in the footsteps of those who were.

The fact that we did not start out personally wealthy may be perceived as a great blessing. To have been born into wealth would have totally obliterated one's opportunity to experience the stimulating challenge of attaining success on their own merit and via their own energy. By starting from scratch, we are afforded the opportunity to prove to ourselves as well as those close to us we are capable of being very successful through our own enterprising efforts. Always remember the journey is definitely more important that the destination and what a wonderful, enlightening, rewarding journey it can be.

Fortunately for us, the students of first generation millionaires, the first subset is by far the largest, comprising over 80% of the current millionaires. There is something about the success stories from those who come from modest to frugal heritage and achieve a level of success with which they are comfortable, that is heartfelt by most everyone. It also serves as proof that if they can do it, it is likely possible for others to attain their goals as well. This is extremely valuable information.

A disproportionate majority of the first generation millionaires owned their own businesses, which they had grown over the years, often from a very modest beginning. Hard work, consistent product or service, accommodating personality, whatever it takes attitude, and a willingness to go the extra mile all seem to add up to a winning combination. Our trip through the pages is not just about how to go about starting a business if you so desire or making your current business more profitable if you already have one, though these topics will be addressed, but it is about what many self made millionaires did that allowed them to attain their station in life. We will not only attempt to explain what they did to achieve their extraordinary success, we will also strive to explain to the best of our ability how they think, which leads them to their successful behavior.

In addition, we will investigate philosophies with regard to savings, investing, habits of decision, use of imagination, goal setting, and instant gratification versus long term thinking, the sincerity and respect with which they serve their customers, and the pride they take in a job well done.

Also we will discover a large majority of those which belong to an elite group we might describe as 'independently wealthy' enjoy themselves so much they are not even aware they are working. Even if they did not have to "go to work" which they don't have to, they would anyway, because they enjoy it so much, and this is exactly what they are doing.

A very long time ago when I was a young child I had a passion to become a millionaire. Little did I know then that a burning desire was the first step in attaining riches. As I grew older and neared maturity, I was constantly intrigued by the realization that some people had reached a level where monetary considerations were not a factor in their lives.

Coming from a modest upbringing, this struck me as almost unbelievable. I was so fascinated by this revelation that it became an obsession. I could walk down the street daydreaming, completely entranced, unaware of friends or family beside me. It seemed nearly impossible that anyone could be in such a delightful financial position.

I was fortunate to be able to start work at an early age. This afforded me an opportunity to begin to get a feel for the value of money. I would weigh an anticipated expenditure over very carefully in my mind prior to parting with my hard-earned cash. Therefore, when I was exposed to people who had little or no concern for the value of money, I was truly intrigued. This was how I wanted to live. However, I had no idea how to get there. It was a goal I very much wanted to achieve.

Many years have passed since those youthful days and I am amazed at the outcome. At the time I was taking the journey, I often felt I was stumbling along the path with no definite direction. In looking back it becomes apparent that the initial burning desire was in command all the way.

When you read the biographies and/or autobiographies of the super successful people, past and current, you often get a glimpse of the passion that drove them to a position where they are towering over others. It is that overwhelming burning desire that dominated their thoughts and emotions on their own personal journeys.

As a national sales manager for a large company, I had the opportunity to study the behavior of over a hundred sales people. I always knew right away when I had a 'winner,' the fellow who came in with a number of orders regularly. Usually one or two of the orders would not meet our credit rating or were cancelled because he tried too hard, but he went out just as cheerfully again the next day. Another fellow, on the other hand, prided himself as never having a cancellation. The only problem, his sales production was very light and we had to let him go. Everybody is going to fail sometimes; it is the one that has the will to succeed and stays the course who will always be the winner.

Keep your mind on your goal and your emotional fortitude will provide the energy necessary for accomplishment. *How the Wealthy Get That Way* will provide interesting insights into ways to proceed on your own unique and exciting journey.

Years ago I was attempting to start a new business. It seemed impossible to put the financing together without my putting up a substantial amount of money. This I didn't have at the time. Attending a lecture on mind control, the speaker asked for a coin (a quarter). He suggested that we all concentrate on how much money we would like to have. Sounding like a game, he further asked us to whisper the amount in our neighbor's ear, and pass the quarter. Well, I knew what I needed, so I whispered the amount, plus 50% just in case something unforeseen happened. You may not believe this, but within 30 days, I had the exact amount and the bank was readying the loan papers. We learn from The Power of Positive Thinking — aiming high is just as easy as aiming low.

This adventure will be one of discovering what techniques, strategies, planning, and foresight have proven successful for those who have already reached and in many cases, exceeded their goals. This path we are about to travel together leads toward wealth.

Pursue it to the degree you desire to succeed. Your effort will be a reflection of what is comfortable and beneficial for your unique set of circumstances.

We will look at philosophies regarding saving and investing. We will study habits of decision making, use of imagination, and goal setting. We will look at the sincerity and respect with which the successful serve their customers, and the pride they take in a job well done. We will compare instant gratification to long-term thinking.

So, welcome to the world of wealth. It requires hard work, discipline, planning, sacrifice, and constant alertness to those opportunities which regularly surround all of us, but it is well worth the effort and an accomplishment you will likely look back on with great pride and joy. It is our sincere desire for you, the reader, the recipient, the customer to benefit in proportion to the effort you are willing to put forth and enjoy the literary journey as much as we did preparing it for you.

Now, with the motivating force of 'That Burning Desire' on our side, let us proceed on our journey by examining two very different types of assets.

YOUR JOURNEY TO FINANCIAL INDEPENDENCE

2

ASSETS

MYSTICALLY INTRIGUING is the phenomenon that some individuals have tremendous earning power and accumulate no significant wealth while others with only a small fraction of their earning capacity attain great nest eggs. This apparent paradox has led to a study the results of which we will share with you.

Everyone's a little different. Just as we are told no two leaves or no two snowflakes are identical, it also holds true that no two people are identical in every respect. Part of what this means in our context is that when it comes to choosing among various potential purchases, and more specifically between those purchases which afford immediate gratification or opting for long range investments which are more compatible with planning toward financial independence down the road or some combination in between, individuals will likely display many different propensities in acting out their personal behavioral choices. Some spend available funds freely on whatever catches their fancy at the moment, apparently very much aware another pay check will be coming in a couple of weeks, while others are very cautious with their money. Since these choices have a profound effect on their eventual financial status, let's look at an example which is demonstrative.

APPRECIATING ASSETS VS. DEPRECIATING ASSETS

Few assets remain at a constant value over time. Most might be expected to decrease in value or increase in value as time marches on. All other factors held constant, to the degree individuals choose more appreciating assets and less depreciating assets, their wealth grows, with the passing of time. And time, like it or not, is an omnipresent constant in the equation of life.

ENTER MORRIE AND MIKE

Let's take a look at a set of twins, Morrie and Mike, who are very similar in many ways but are not identical. The physician who delivered them called them mirror image twins. They had a great time growing up together. Their parents could tell them apart, but their teachers and friends from visual input were clueless with respect to which one of the twins they were addressing. However, when it came to personalities, much individuality was observed. For instance, Morrie was very meticulous about his dress and grooming, while Mike would let his hair fly in the breeze and remark, "seeing which way my hair is going is how I know which way the wind is blowing." They also have different propensities with respect to their financial instincts. They have grown up together in a modest, but loving environment and are very much alike in many ways, especially their looks, but as they approach maturity their differences become more and more apparent. Mike is very outgoing, has lots of friends constantly around and is known as the life of the party. His major focus in life has to do with 'where's the party tonight.' Morrie tends to be a little quieter, more reserved and you might even say analytical in his demeanor. He tends to concern himself more with the future than with immediate pleasures.

As luck would have it, one day shortly after their nineteenth birthday they received the devastating news that their long lost Aunt Pauline, the obstetrician from Philadelphia, had died and left them each $50,000 cash. The twins were ecstatic! They had only met Aunt Pauline one time when they were quite young. She had never married and had been so consumed with her medical practice she seldom communicated. The twins had more or less forgotten she existed. That was until this news arrived! Oh yes! Wow! Sure they remembered their dear old Aunt Pauline. And such a shame she passed on!

What happens next is of major interest. Mike, after little thought, goes shopping and buys himself a beautiful new red luxury sports coupe. He is the talk of the town. He and his friends have a blast with the shiny new vehicle, and friends galore, even more than before. Mike felt this was the best purchase he had ever made. He took very good care of his new car, washing and polishing it daily. And since there was a little of Aunt Pauline's money left, he bought a few fancy accessories to make it even snappier than it originally appeared on the showroom floor.

Morrie, being much more conservative and long range in his thinking, was content to drive his somewhat dilapidated pickup truck and invest his fifty grand in the stock market. Morrie spent considerable time and effort studying the stock market and made some well thought out decisions. The vicissitudinous stock market had many ups and downs over the next twenty years. However, Morrie remained steadfast to his basic investment principles. Morrie was a meticulous record keeper and had constant statistics, graphs, and charts on his investments. Morrie's assets, under his careful guidance, grew at an average rate of twenty percent for twenty years.

So twenty years after the sad day when dear old Aunt Pauline passed on, Mike's luxury car had depreciated to zero. As a matter of fact, it went to its final resting place in the local salvage yard 8½ years prior, while Morrie's investment portfolio had grown to $1,916,000.00. Nearly two million dollars!

This illustrates the dramatic difference between Mike's depreciating automobile and Morrie's appreciating stock market portfolio.

Which twin in your opinion made the wiser choice? The 39 year old with negligible net worth or the 39 year old multimillionaire?

The following discussion of appreciating and depreciating assets will present generalities for which there admittedly exist many exceptions. For example, we will speak of automobiles as depreciating assets and one may point out the antique car buff who purchases an antique or classic automobile which has been abandoned and laid to rest in the farmer's field. He fixes it up like new, spending hundreds or thousands of hours on the restoration and makes some money on the sale of the car. This may amount to twenty five or fifty cents an hour or less for the time expended. Also when we look at real estate as an appreciating asset, one might bring attention to the astute homeowner who does his homework and purchases the best bargain in real estate right before the real estate crash in Texas or Arizona or any other of many locations and loses considerable money on what is ordinarily considered to be an appreciating asset. Also, some may have strong opinions and experiences to back their claim that much money can and has been made (or lost) in coins, stamps, art, gold, silver, and tons of commodities as well as many other items. These are all true and can be documented in both directions. None of these facts are in any way disputed, but it is far beyond the scope of this book to discuss any or all of these truths. Instead it is our goal to provide an elementary framework for spotting what are generally considered appreciating and depreciating assets to the previously unordained. Our apologies are extended to those who view this discussion as superficial or shallow, but our intention is to point out concepts of growing vs. shrinking assets and to the extent that has been accomplished, this section has been successful.

For the purpose of our discussion we will identify:

APPRECIATING ASSETS as those assets which can be logically expected to be worth more in the future. They are customarily thought of as: well-selected stocks, bonds, mutual funds, treasury bills, or real estate.

DEPRECIATING ASSETS are assets which are likely to be worth substantially less in the future. They are automobiles, boats, airplanes, motorcycles, televisions, household furnishings, wardrobes, computers, expendables, consumables, anything with tires, propellers, or internal combustion engines.

Used cars, boats, trucks, four-wheelers, snowmobiles, along with all other similar items generally can be expected to bring less in the marketplace than do new items. For instance, if you were to purchase a new pickup truck, drive it around the block, then decide to sell it for some undisclosed reason, you would likely get considerably less (probably measured in thousands of dollars) than you initially paid. Your pickup may even have less miles on its odometer than some of the 'new' pickups on the dealer's showroom floor, but what you can recover is much less, simply because it is considered a second-hand vehicle.

This is not saying never buy a new vehicle. It is suggesting, be aware of the consequences of buying a new vehicle and figure a significant decline in value for that first 'drive around the block.'

Many very successful wealth accumulators have reported various alternatives to buying new vehicles which may or may not be compatible with your particular desires, propensities, or psychological makeup. One popular strategy is to purchase three or four year old luxury automobiles (often dealers program cars) for in the vicinity of half of the car's original 'sticker price.' While these automobiles are indeed depreciating during the accumulators ownership, the depreciation is at a much lower rate and does not include the initial new car drop in value. Others bought dealers demonstration models at a steep discount. Still others spoke of finding a make, model, and year they wanted, and then watching the newspaper advertisements for an owners desperation plea. "Must sell," "take over payments," "been given a company car," "need to sell like new such and such model," "leaving country, took a job overseas, must sell today!" etc. In the 'take over payments' situation, the accumulator would not actually take over the payments, but might, however, negotiate a cash price from either the owner or the finance company which is 'holding the bag' on the vehicle. When the owner is having a rough time keeping current on their payments, it may soften the lien holder's position as they might well view their alternative option of repossessing and selling the automobile as quite expensive.

Finding the right automobile at the right price is not usually an easy task. Quite often it is time consuming and consists of looking at scores of automobiles and negotiating with dozens of owners. However, these successful wealth accumulators usually arrive at some great deals and the best part is that they seem to love the satisfaction which comes from finding outstanding values and negotiating the purchase.

Though much time may be spent, it is viewed as a hobby or recreational adventure which is thoroughly enjoyed by the purchaser. There certainly are hobbies which are less desirable and more monetarily derogative.

The same applies, sometimes to a greater or lesser extent, to all other depreciating assets. For instance, if one were to see a beautiful bedroom set priced at $6200 which they could not live without, and were able to negotiate the salesman down to $5250 delivered, and for some unknown reason decided to sell it the next week, it is doubtful that by placing an advertisement in the newspaper ($35.00 expense) one could get more than $2500 the following week for the 'used' bedroom set. Similar scenarios would be likely with other furniture purchases.

A custom tailored men's suit presents an interesting example. The next day after paying $675 for the beautiful suit, resale value is approaching zero were one in the selling mode.

The message is not "don't buy furniture or clothes." Rather the point is to begin to grasp the contrast between appreciating and depreciating assets.

Obviously we regularly choose many assets which have little value soon after their purchase, which we feel are a good value to us because they suit our current or ongoing needs or desires. This is to be expected and looked on with favor as all the assets we choose to purchase cannot and should not necessarily be appreciating assets.

If you don't purchase any expendables in our society you probably don't survive very long. However, when people habitually spend all available funds on expendables to the extreme that no savings for appreciating assets are available, their long term prospects for attaining financial freedom are obviously greatly reduced.

The contrasting behaviors in the management of money displayed by Morrie and Mike is an extreme example for the purpose of illustrating an important point. However, in our routine day to day transactions, those who have a tendency to defer the immediate pleasure for the long term reward (drive the old pickup and buy stocks) tend to realize far greater benefits in later years than those less disciplined who tend to opt for the immediate pleasure (sports car) which would have been available earlier (at the time of their inheritance).

The propensity to spend freely or to save tends to be inherent in most individuals and is altered only with significant conscious effort in the majority of people studied. It goes without saying, the vast majority of self-made millionaires have a strong tendency to defer the immediate rewards in favor of long term benefits. They appear to have a built in sixth sense about the direction the value of their purchases will be headed in the intermediate to long term.

Benefits are difficult to weigh and are obviously very subjective in nature. All individuals possess their own unique value system and therefore will rate all aspects of their being and surroundings quite differently. Morrie was obtaining much joy from watching his nest egg grow, and Mike was undoubtedly receiving significant pleasure from his snappy sports car and the throng of friends it attracted, though at some point he was likely quite chagrin as he realized his asset was depreciating or had depreciated to zero as Morrie's assets continued to grow.

'Twenty-twenty hindsight' is what has been referred to as 'perfect vision.' When we are able to anticipate the likely 'value down the road' of a purchase made today, we are in a much better position to evaluate the choices we make. Today for instance, the thirty-nine year old Mike says, "I certainly wish I had invested my inheritance like Morrie did instead of buying that sports car." The thirty-nine year old Morrie says, "I am very happy with my choice to invest my inheritance." Knowing these outcomes prior to facing one's daily choices is to some degree instructive for those yet to be encountered decisions which are inherent in our lifetimes.

EFFECTS OF TIME ON ASSETS

Time is a constant which is marching on at a steady pace. It is entirely up to us whether we put it to work for us or let it work against us. We can go with the grain and see how wonderful life can be or we can choose to go against the grain and struggle with life.

The goal of this chapter is to take a look at choices of various assets and observe how these choices work out in the long run. Was the pleasure of blitzing down the street in the shiny new coupe, which is now worth nothing, equal to the multi-million dollar nest egg at present? Framed this way, at this point in time, probably not. However, twenty years prior the answer may not have been so obvious. This is what we will be doing, taking a glance into the future and making an educated guess as to the probable outcome of our various choices. Our auto versus stock example is pretty clean cut and obvious, but there are many much more subtle choices which we all face regularly that are not so crystal clear. Our ability to recognize appreciating asset versus depreciating asset tendencies in our daily encounters can have significant impact on our financial future.

A question one may choose to ask of all potential purchases is, "Will this purchase be worth zero one day?" When the answer is yes, it may deserve a second look prior to proceeding. Obviously we will find it beneficial if not absolutely necessary to complete many of these transactions, however, awareness of the inevitable valueless-ness of the purchase may help avoid some tempting uses of capital which might be better utilized in other ways. The compounded effect over a substantial period of time of investing in appreciating assets, those funds which might have been squandered by the less informed or less disciplined, can and will have a phenomenal impact on long term net worth. Just as the acorn planted in youth and cared for and protected along with regular watering, grows to be a mighty oak tree, so do savings added to regularly and cultivated to a healthy growth-inducing environment flourish into substantial wealth.

The formula is very simple: *the sooner and more invested in appreciating assets, the quicker the financial freedom is realized.* First we must learn to recognize assets which are likely to grow. Second we must display discipline to acquire these growing assets and add to them regularly.

Once one has made the commitment to invest, much informa-tion is available in the library, on the internet, or from many other sources. The key in this information age is the willingness to put forth the necessary effort to seek out the available information and process it in order to come to some favorable investment decisions.

There is no excuse for the investor to not be well informed on his own behalf, as nothing will ever take the place of personal responsi-bility for ones own actions. You simply must do the work to assure yourself of the continuing rewards. If it is real estate you are inter-ested in, you must follow local as well as regional and national trends, look at a lot of properties, get to know many people in the field and in general eat, drink, and sleep real estate. One of the respected real estate gurus once stated "prior to making an offer on a house, look at at least one hundred similarly priced homes in your target area. By the time you have carefully analyzed one hundred similar properties, you are the expert on value." This may seem to some like it is asking a lot, however this serious of a commitment for your hard earned cash deserves your extreme effort, and your long term rewards for a job well done tend to be commensurate with the effort expended.

Real estate agents may be of some help, but it remains your responsibility to determine the real value of your purchase. The real estate agent receives a commission on any property she sells you, as she well should, but impact of a forthcoming commission could possibly in some cases have at least a slight influence on her view of the transaction.

Appraisals may be of value, however, remember one appraisal definition goes something like, "that price a seller that is not under duress and a willing and able buyer agree on." So, as you can imagine from your personal experiences with a wide assortment of people, some sales prices are quite unrelated to actual value. Also be aware that by signing a purchase agreement, you may be leading an appraiser to a number which would not otherwise have been attained.

Similarly if stocks and bonds are where your interests lie, there are many excellent sources of information available. Also stockbrokers can assist you, but once again some might tend to be influenced by their potential for commission. The responsibility for your expenditures once again rests solely on your shoulders. This is not to say that after your confidence has been earned by a competent stock broker you cannot take their recommendations seriously. The point being, 'if you lose your shirt in the market, it's your fault for listening, not theirs for advising!" It's a tough pill to swallow, but that is the way it is.

Whatever appreciating assets you choose as your route to financial freedom, learn all you can, from as many sources as available. Seek the opinions of respected authorities. Study conflicting evidence to determine which is more nearly correct or consistent with the other information you have gleaned. On the basis of your extensive research, make your own decisions! The longer you pursue the area of your investments, the more you learn and therefore, the more competent and successful you likely will become. It's all right to start out slowly and build a good foundation of knowledge and experience from which to operate. As you become more and more comfortable in your chosen field you can intelligently and confidently increase your position.

In time your assets grow and your competence to achieve greater returns increases; the combination is exhilarating, affording still more effort and further success. This is what is called the spiral effect. Hard work begets success which increases enthusiasm which increases efforts which begets more success. The spiral effect, either positive or negative, is commonly at work in our lives. When negative, stop it in its tracks, when positive, ride the wave to the maximum.

3

INTEREST

A powerful source and one you want on your side.

FULL AND THOROUGH understanding, appreciation, and respect for interest is most beneficial and some would even say manditory if one is to ascend to the financial elite status desired by so many. Interest can be likened to a head wind or a tailwind in aeronautical terms, or to an uphill versus a downhill journey to the ground traveler, or high seas as opposed to calm waters to the nautically oriented. The point is that interest can be going out, a heavy burden on your wealth accumulation, or it can be coming in, a tremendous benefit on your journey toward financial freedom. Being constantly aware of what factor interest is playing in your financial scheme is critically important. The more interest we manage to get coming in and the less going out the more able we are to navigate in calm seas where much progress toward our desired financial destination is possible.

HOME MORTGAGES

Home mortgages specifically, and real estate mortgages in general, are some of the major causes of interest outflow in most families' financial scenario. Anything which can be done to favorably alter this tremendous long term commitment has potential for heroic rewards. This is an excellent time to get the creative juices flowing and come up with money saving ideas.

Real estate transactions are serious, cumbersome, and expensive commitments. It is imperative that you are represented by an attorney when entering into any real estate agreements. Following will be some views for you to discuss with your attorney to see if any are applicable to your situation.

Granted, home mortgages are often essential and make good financial sense for most of us. However, some scenarios where on top of a 30 year mortgage, costly second and at times third mortgages get stacked, and the uncanny homeowner may pay three, four, or even five or six times the initial purchase price of the house in interest payments. This is the antithesis of wealth accumulation, and is most likely to end in a deep dark place where no one desires to be financially. Add to this credit card balances at 18% to 21% and soon Mr. Naive is spinning his wheels and digging himself a very deep financial hole as his monthly interest payments are approaching his monthly income and escape appears impossible.

Please don't get the wrong impression, home mortgages are a part of life, but paying them back in 15 years, or even 10 years instead of the traditional 30 years will turn the interest tide in your favor much sooner. The less time you use the lender's money, the less interest you pay. In summary, borrow the least amount of money at the lowest possible interest rate for the shortest time period. Period!

To get a better grasp of the magnitude and significance of this important interest factor, let's look into a typical home mortgage. A 30 year home mortgage for $200,000 at 9½% when it runs full term results in the mortgagee paying a total of $603,450 during the course of the contract. Those unfortunate enough to be paying 11% fork out $678,108 in repaying the $200,000 borrowed.

So in actuality, the homeowner is paying, on average, at a ratio of approximately $1 toward the house and $2 to the mortgage company every time the payment is made for thirty years. No wonder this mortgage balance goes down so slowly.

Since mortgages are such a huge expense in our own personal macro economy, let's take a look at possible alternatives. Anything which has the potential to lower the interest rate, decrease or eliminate the initiation fees, or shorten the term of the mortgage is well worth investigating.

BORROWING FUNDS FROM A RELATIVE OR FRIENDS

Though borrowing from friends and relatives is customarily not recommended, situations at times exist where it can make sense and actually be turned into a win-win situation. For instance, if you have a retiring relative or friend, let's say Uncle Ralph, who might otherwise be looking into some safe and conservative investment like treasury bills at the time when you are in the process of buying a house, you might be able to negotiate a deal where you put the house up as security and Uncle Ralph furnishes the money to purchase the house and receives 1.5% more interest than the going treasury bill rate. Uncle Ralph has known you since you were born and is totally comfortable with the fact that you are very responsible. Also, he is pleased to be able to help you get started in your first home. Your side of the equation might be that you avoid mortgage initiation fees, which are typically measured in the thousands of dollars and get an interest rate a point or two less than current mortgage rates, which is hugely beneficial. Uncle Ralph receives his monthly check to live on, along with a note from his favorite nephew. Since your interest payment is considerably less you may be able to pay off the loan in far fewer years which saves even more of your hard earned cash.

SELLER FINANCING

Another alternative may be for the seller to finance your purchase. When you find a motivated seller who has no immediate need for cash or does not need all of his cash at the time of the sale, it may be possible to negotiate a sale where the seller agrees to "carry back" the mortgage or a portion of it. What this means is the seller agrees to accept monthly payments from you rather than requiring all his money at the time of the sale. In this scenario it is important to be certain there is a clause which states that there is no prepayment penalty, so you can pay your obligation in full as soon as possible when your opportunity presents itself.

BROKERAGE ACCOUNTS

Once you have attained sufficient equity in a brokerage account (stocks, mutual funds, bonds) it is possible to borrow against your equity at a rate which is customarily significantly below current mortgage rates. And once again you avoid the huge mortgage initiation fees.

ANY OTHER SOURCES AVAILABLE TO YOU

Each individual's situation is unique and therefore at times presents its own opportunities. Pursue all possible avenues as any unconventional means of financing your home will likely save you considerable money in the long term. For instance, some employers have been known to have funds available for employees to use when purchasing homes. Perhaps a professional organization, labor union, credit union or social organization in your area has or knows of some alternative source of funding. Pursue any and all leads aggressively.

The argument is consistently made that the mortgage interest is tax deductible, so don't worry about it. It may be true that it is tax deductible, however, the less interest you pay, the more money you have, period! Some of your friends who are advising you may be to the point where they are owing more interest than their income can support. Thankfully you know better.

CREDIT CARDS

Did you ever wonder why when you enter certain department stores, the 'greeters' attempt to tackle you and give you free gifts and discounts if you will only sign up for their credit card? Well the answer is PROFIT. Studying the financials of some of the mega retailers reveals the profit from interest earned on their credit cards exceeds their profit from merchandise sales! No wonder they are so anxious to issue as many credit cards as possible. The reason this is such a profit center is twofold. One factor is the astronomical interest rates charged on the outstanding balance (18% to 22%). The other is the human propensity of many in our current society to spend huge amounts of money when they have credit cards at their disposal. The little plastic card with a $300 or $500 or $1000 or $3000 or $10,000 limit appears to have the same effect as cash in the pockets of some customers. It's like the credit card needs to be 'maxed out' or it might burn a hole in their wallet. This spendthrift mind set comes in varying degrees and is significantly more prevalent than would be expected of otherwise rationally acting customers.

And then, as if things were not bad enough already, at the end of the billing cycle when the statement is sent to the credit card holder, the shrewd creditor suggests a minimal payment, typically 2% of the outstanding balance, which serves to maximize the future interest. Interestingly enough, a very high percentage of cardholders for some reason follow the suggestion and make the minimum payment. This is financial suicide! The card holder's philosophy appears to be, "conserve money for the moment by paying the minimum and don't worry about the remaining balance. The balance we can worry about later." The part that is not comprehended is the effect of the horrendous interest accumulation on the unpaid balance. For instance, when the minimal payment is 2% per month, as the interest rate being charged approaches 24% the number of payments approaches infinity. No depletion of the principal is occurring. At 22% interest and paying 2% of the balance monthly, it could take most of a lifetime to get the balance paid in full. And that is if no further charges were made on the credit card. What a self defeating way to spend your money and your life.

Another example is if you put a $1000 charge on your credit card for a kayak you just couldn't resist and your credit card company is charging only 18% interest, your first minimum payment will be 2% of $1000 or $20. If you continue to pay the industry standard 2% minimum, it will take 19 years and 4 months to repay your debt. The interest you will pay in that time will be a horrifying $1,931.06. So you pay for the kayak nearly three times and only get one kayak.

Credit cards are fine, *as long as you pay your balance in full prior to the time when any interest has been charged*. Credit cards are a legitimate tool when used for their convenience. If you have a credit card for the purpose of using your available balance as a source of money, you are making a terrible choice as to where to borrow money. Credit cards are historically known for their astronomical interest rates and there is no reason to expect any significant change in the near future. In addition, other charges and penalties added, such as late payments and/or over limit fees, from time to time make a bad situation even worse. Simply put, 'pay off your entire balance prior to interest charges accruing or cut them up.' You work too hard for your money to be paying twenty something percent interest on an outstanding balance on your credit cards.

Wherever you are paying interest of any kind, explore possibilities for eliminating the interest in the near future. If it's not possible to eliminate the interest, take a close look at possibilities of reducing the rate of interest as well as decreasing the time until the obligation is eliminated. The sooner you eliminate the interest obligation, the sooner your financial ship experiences smooth sailing toward your financial goals.

PUTTING INTEREST TO WORK FOR YOU

Now that we are aware of how devastating interest can be, let's take a look at the flip side of the interest story. This is interest which is being paid to you. *That wonderful tailwind!* This interest can be from mortgages you own on real estate, maybe you 'carried back' on a property you sold, secured loans owed you, treasury bills, money market accounts, interest from savings accounts, or many other sources. When the interest coming in exceeds the interest going out, your interest factor is positive. If this is your current situation, congratulations! If it is not, keep constantly aware of how you might be able to turn it around as soon as possible.

It is recommended that at least annually, and more often if your financial picture is in a state of flux, you do an interest analysis in order to be aware of your interest factor score. For your convenience in calculating your current interest status see figure 3-1. This can be a monthly calculation, say for December 2003 or an annual figure, whichever is more convenient for you. Be sure to note the date and retain your interest factor analysis for future reference so you can monitor your progress and improvement in making life easier for yourself. Periodic review of your interest factor analysis will assist you in confirming you are headed in the right direction by showing

Figure 3.1 — INTEREST FACTOR ANALYSIS

Time period month _____   Year ended _____

INTEREST PAID
Home Mortgage .... _____
2nd Mortgage .... _____
Other Mortgages .... _____
_____ .... _____

Credit Cards
Visa .... _____
Master Card .... _____
Discover .... _____
American Express.... _____
Sears .... _____
_____ .... _____
_____ .... _____

Auto Loans
_____ .... _____
_____ .... _____
_____ .... _____

Toys
Boat .... _____
Motorcycle .... _____
Snowmobile .... _____
_____ .... _____
_____ .... _____
_____ .... _____

Total Paid .... _____

INTEREST RECEIVED
Mortgages Held...... _____
_____ .... _____
_____ .... _____
_____ .... _____

Stocks and Bonds
_____ .... _____
_____ .... _____
_____ .... _____
_____ .... _____
_____ .... _____
_____ .... _____

Mutual Funds
_____ .... _____
_____ .... _____
_____ .... _____
_____ .... _____

Loans Receivable
_____ .... _____
_____ .... _____
_____ .... _____
Other_____ .... _____
_____ .... _____

Total Received .... _____

Minus Total Interest Paid .... _____

THE INTEREST FACTOR (+ for positive, - for negative) _____

a steady improvement in your interest factor status.

WOW! What a revealing exercise! These numbers explain the role interest is playing in your financial picture. This is where the interest money is coming from or going. Hopefully you have positioned yourself so the playing field is tipped in your favor (more interest coming in than going out). If this is the case, remain constantly on the look out for additional means by which you can further improve your interest factor position. Regular savings, well secured loans, mortgages in your favor, or any other means of increasing the flow of interest in your direction makes life so much more enjoyable.

All other factors held constant, and with the same monthly income, imagine the contrasting lifestyles between the family traveling against the grain (paying out $1,000 interest a month) and the family traveling with the grain (receiving $1,000 interest a month). These differences don't just happen. They are the result of conscious choices on the part of the 'actors' on the stage of life. Those who play out their roles by accumulating a collection of credit cards which they feel compelled to 'max out' and choose to make minimum monthly payments on their outstanding balances are setting the stage for fighting the up hill battle. And as is readily apparent and straight forward, when framed this way, the financially astute individual who pays the full balance on his credit cards and chooses options which can earn him the right to receive interest on a regular and ongoing basis is paving the way for his journey on the high road to financial independence.

On the other hand, if the interest factor analysis shows a strong negative balance, it is most beneficial to become aware of one of the major factors which has been responsible for the 'tough sledding' you have been experiencing in your financial struggle to make ends meet. If this is your situation, don't despair, it just means it is homework time. If it is credit cards which are causing the problem as is often the case, be thankful the cause has been discovered so you can start doing something which will lead to resolving the problem. You cannot solve the problem until you understand what the problem is. Get out a sheet of paper and list each credit card along with the outstanding balance and the interest being charged on that outstanding balance. Now, your top priority must be to eliminate credit card debt beginning with the highest interest rate cards first. Draw a line in the sand as this is the date when you no longer make any charges on your credit cards and the only transactions are payments which reduce your balances! If it is possible to pay the credit card balances in full in three or four months, go for it. Do not overlook the possibility of a second or third job, the entire proceeds of which go directly toward reducing credit card balances. Many of us have held down three or four jobs at the same time and have apparently turned out no worse for the experience. If you have dug such a deep hole it is not possible to recover in a few months, then after vowing to make no more charges, start paying on the highest interest cards first while you are looking for alternative sources of lower interest money. This might be a loan from a credit union or bank or a debt consolidation loan at perhaps half the interest rate you are paying on your credit cards. At any rate, it is mandatory to eliminate your high interest debt as soon as possible. Then make a vow to never go back to that high interest debt place again.

The lower interest rate loan to pay off the credit cards is a means to an end and not an end in itself. What this means is that interest is still being charged albeit at a lower rate so the new loan should be retired in as few months as possible. Plan your debt attack to pay the loan off in five or six months or if your debt is extreme, nine to twelve months. Tell the lender you intend to pay your obligation back in say six months and see what your monthly payments will be. This dictates how many extra jobs you take on in the meantime. Paying a little more than the minimum will give you a great feeling of accomplishment and cut down on the interest going out.

Interest rates vary considerably over time and many debt consolidation programs come and go. As of this writing, MBNA (phone number 1-800-527-3621) is advertising a disappearing debt program with annual percentage rates from 12.99% to 18.99% based on your credit worthiness. These loans are for amounts up to $25,000. We sincerely hope you don't need that much. Their advertising, of course, assumes you qualify for the 12.99%, which in actuality you may or may not. This is longer term and higher interest than we would hope you can negotiate. However, it will at least serve as a reference point and hopefully a poor alternative to your options.

— Disappearing debt loan of $5,000
    Payment: $141 for 48 months
             $177 for 36 months

— Disappearing debt loan of $10,000
    Payment: $239 for 60 months
             $281 for 48 months
             $353 for 36 months

— Disappearing debt loan of $15,000
    Payment: $316 for 72 months
             $358 for 60 months
             $442 for 48 months
             $530 for 36 months

— Disappearing debt loan of $20,000
   Payment: $421 for 72 months
           $477 for 60 months
           $563 for 48 months
           $707 for 36 months

— Disappearing debt loan of $25,000
   Payment: $527 for 72 months
           $597 for 60 months
           $703 for 48 months
           $883 for 36 months

We have no affiliation with MBNA and are not recommending you use their services. This is purely presented as an example of what is currently being advertised. In our opinion lower interest loans are likely available from other sources. The point is if you have high interest debt it is essential for you to establish a plan to make it disappear as soon as possible.

Once the credit card dilemma is corrected, go directly to work on any other debt, leaving the typically low interest first mortgage on your home until last. In some rare cases if interest rates have risen substantially since your fixed rate home mortgage was initiated and you safely receive a higher interest rate from other sources than you pay on your home mortgage, it may make sense to make minimum mortgage payments. Pencil out the various options and proceed as the numbers direct you.

Life is much more enjoyable after you have worked your way out of debt. It may take a while and require sacrifices along the way, but the rewards are well worth the effort expended. Congratulations on your decision to be debt free!

RULE OF 72

Interest received is a valuable resource of income for those who have arranged their finances in such a way as to be primarily on the receiving end of the interest equation. The rule of 72 states that the number of years necessary for your principle to double in value can be found by dividing your current interest rate into the number 72. The quotient is the number of years to double. Therefore if you are earning 8% interest on your savings, you divide 8 into 72 and determine in nine years your principle will double. A conservative investor choosing a 6% return would double his principle in twelve years. At 24% interest your principle doubles in three years. Therefore those acquaintances of yours (I'm sure you know better) who maintain a credit card balance of $10,000 at 24% for three years accumulate an additional $10,000 worth of interest in this time period. This is $10,000 they pay the credit card company for which they receive no tangible goods. Such silly friends you have! It's wonderful you know better.

INVESTMENT PORTFOLIO RETURNS

Likely, anticipated, forecasted, hoped for, and real earnings have varied immensely over the years, from some devastatingly negative figures in the great depression of the 1930's when some investors saw as much as 70% to 90% of their portfolios disappear, to some huge gains in happier times. By dividing, let's say, 15% into 72 we learn that in a little less than 5 years one would be able to double one's principle. Super savvy investors in some good times have reported some sustained bursts of earnings in the vicinity of 24%. These fortunate individuals during these periods of high earnings see their nest eggs double in three years.

In this hypothetical case, the investor with one million dollars gains the second million in only three years. Perhaps the first million took him twenty years. Accumulation of the second million came much easier indeed, and much faster. If the following three years were equally as good, he might gain two million in the next three years. The more principle assets the investor has available for growth, the faster the new earnings are attained. This may be one reason for the old adage that "The first million is the hardest." Another factor is that experience gained in building the first million is hugely beneficial when investing in the future. Once you 'know the ropes,' playing the financial game becomes much easier.

4

YOUR NET WORTH

"Make it thy business to know thyself,
which is the most difficult lesson in the world."
                                                    Cervantes

NOW THAT WE SEE the role interest plays in our financial well being, it's time to look at net worth. Net worth is an accounting term of vital interest to bankers and loan officers. They will evaluate your financial strength, as a customer and/or potential customer, by your net worth. Financially secure individuals monitor these figures closely, for it tells them what the current score is in the financial game in which we are all participants, whether we know it or not. I calculate my net worth quarterly and since you are interested in joining the ranks of the financially independent, it's time for you to get to work on yours.

What is this net worth anyway? Simply put, it is the difference between everything you own minus everything you owe, or in accounting terms, all your assets minus all your debt. To arrive at this magic number we use a Personal Financial Statement, which is typically a two-page form which can be obtained from any bank or stationary store.

Joann L. Burrough of Michigan State University is the author of a very good personal financial statement. If you have a computer, you can download it from: www.nemonline.org/bus_plan/fin_state.html or for your convenience a typical financial statement form can be found at the end of this chapter.

I strongly suggest you print out a couple of copies as worksheets. Once you have compiled your data, you may consider setting up on Excel's spreadsheet your customized version of a financial statement, which will automatically give you your net worth.

Take a good look at Ms. Burrough's form. The first thing you see is, "As of _____20__". You must pick a date that will indicate the date of this statement. Typically one uses a month-end, or a year-end like Dec. 31 2003. Most likely some of the pertinent figures you will need won't be available until the following 10th of the month. Bank, broker and credit card statements may be needed to complete the form.

Look at the assets and liabilities section. You will notice that most entries require a description in a section designated by a number. This is where you start. Dig out all of the information asked for and write it in as accurately as possible. Most of us have the tendency to think rather highly of our assets and assign them a greater value than their true market value. Be realistic when it comes to real estate, cars, boats and personal property. Check what homes in your immediate area are selling for, and look at the Sunday newspapers to get a better feeling for current used car, boat, or real estate values. Remember these are asking prices, therefore actual sales prices will usually be somewhat lower.

If there is not enough room on the form, use a yellow pad to list the individual items and then summarize them on the appropriate line. This is a very good time to analyze your assets and liabilities as they are listed and see what can be done to improve your financial position. Can your liabilities be paid off faster perhaps? Can the accounts receivables be collected more aggressively, or can you take advantage of discounts on accounts payable? Are there expenses that could be eliminated? Could you sell that seldom-used item you still owe money on? Or sell the debt-free seldom used item and put the money in the bank?

The last thing is to total the assets side and the liabilities side of the form and finally subtract total liabilities from total assets. This will be your net worth. Here's hoping yours is a positive number, and bigger is much better. When evaluating a client, banks and loan officers like to see a substantial positive number in the net worth slot. You too, will like to see your net worth steadily increase as a result of your efforts and smart investments.

However, could this be a negative number? You bet and here is how it can happen. In our society credit is given too easily to almost everyone. All sorts of incentives are created to lure the unwary into spending money they cannot afford, such as free gifts for signing up, an additional discount on today's purchase, etc.

My 17-year-old granddaughter applied for a Gold American Express card and sure enough she received one in a couple of weeks. Hurrah, big mall here she comes on a big spending spree. What a life, no money, just a plastic card. The day of reckoning came when the statement arrived and neither parents nor grandparents offered to help, but suggested maybe a job and a pair of scissors were in order. The damage was not too great and a good lesson was learned.

Unfortunately, too many folks never come to grips with easy credit. Read the Legal Notices in your daily newspaper and check out the bankruptcy filings. You will be astounded that people with assets of $15,000 have liabilities of $175,000 dollars. How can that be? Easy credit. What a way to live.

Think for a moment of how some of your acquaintances (not you of course, as you are much more financially astute) have managed to record a negative net worth. One possible contributing factor might be buying a new automobile with little or no down payment. This can create a negative net worth very quickly, for the new automobile is probably depreciating faster than the payments are decreasing the outstanding balance. This is particularly the case when the automobile owner consistently puts a lot of miles on the automobile. In this situation, where someone owes more money on a vehicle than could be realized from the sale, it is called it being "upside down in the vehicle". Even if they were to sell the automobile at current market prices, they would not realize enough to pay off their loan.

Unfortunately, vehicles are not the only way to create negative balances on a financial statement. Investments in the stock market will fluctuate in volatile times. The value of your home can also change as real estate is subject to changes. Values can go both up and down. But remember, you don't lose money on your investments or your home, unless you are selling them in a down market. As an investment, real estate will sometimes be trickier to sell in a down market, for it's harder to find a buyer. Your broker, as you know by now, can sell your stock market investments in seconds by telephone. Or you can do it yourself on-line if something troubles you.

If you are a long-term investor, as we hope you are, fluctuations like this should not create a panic situation, but stimulate realistic evaluation of the underlying reason for the down turn. Then you can take appropriate action based on facts. No one can consistently predict accurately all price movements. Usually the best solution is to ride out the volatile times. Historically, charts of most investments show an upward movement over time. People with little risk tolerance are seldom financially successful.

So although negative net worth situations may occasionally appear, the financially resourceful strive to keep their net worth solidly in the plus column. If you were honest with yourself, you obtained an accurate realistic evaluation of your present financial position. Do update your personal financial statement at least annually at the end of the calendar year. A series of these statements over the years will be greatly beneficial in seeing your progress and projecting future net worth. Now let us study financial momentum, discussed in the next chapter.

Personal Financial Statement

CONTACT YOUR REPRESENTATIVE AT THE BANK
IF YOU HAVE ANY QUESTIONS REGARDING THE
COMPLETION OF THIS FORM

YOU MAY APPLY FOR A CREDIT EXTENSION OR FINANCIAL ACCOMMODATION INDIVIDUALLY OR JOINTLY WITH A CO-APPLICANT. THIS STATEMENT AND ANY APPLICABLE SUPPORTING SCHEDULES MAY BE COMPLETED JOINTLY BY BOTH MARRIED AND UNMARRIED CO-APPLICANTS IF THEIR ASSETS AND LIABILITIES ARE SUFFICIENTLY JOINED SO THAT THE STATEMENT CAN BE MEANINGFULLY AND FAIRLY PRESENTED ON A COMBINED BASIS; OTHERWISE SEPARATE STATEMENTS AND SCHEDULES ARE REQUIRED.

APPLICANT

NAME_____ Social Security # _____

ADDRESS_____

TELEPHONE NUMBER_____DATE OF BIRTH_____

PRESENT EMPLOYER_____POSITION _____

ADDRESS_____

CO-APPLICANT

NAME_____ Social Security # _____

ADDRESS_____

TELEPHONE NUMBER_____DATE OF BIRTH_____

PRESENT EMPLOYER_____POSITION _____

ADDRESS_____

DATE OF VALUATION_____

● Round all amounts to the nearest $100
● Attach separate sheet if you need more space to complete detail schedule

ASSETS	AMOUNT	LIABILITIES	AMOUNT
Cash in this Bank	I I	Notes Payable Banks (Schedule 7)	I I
Cash in Other Banks (Detail)	I I	Notes Payable Others (Schedule 7)	I I
	I I	Installment Contracts Payable (Schedule 7)	I I
	I I	Due Dept. Stores, Credit Cards & Others	I I
	I I		I I
Due from Friends, Relatives & Others (Sched. 1)	I I	Income Taxes Payable	I I
	I I		I I
Mortgage & Contracts for Deed Owned (Sched. 2)	I I	Other Taxes Payable	I I
Securities Owned (Schedule 3)	I I		I I
Cash Surrender Value of Life Insur. (Sched. 4)	I I	Loans on Life Insurance (Schedule 4)	I I
Homestead (Schedule 5)	I I		I I
Other Real Estate Owned (Schedule 5)	I I	Mortgage on Homestead (Schedule 6)	I I
Automobiles	I I	Mortgage or Liens on Other Real Estate	I I
	I I	Owned (Schedule 6)	I I
	I I		I I
Personal Property	I I	Other Liabilities (Detail)	I I
	I I		I I
	I I		I I
Other Assets (Detail)	I I		I I
	I I	TOTAL LIABILITIES	I I
	I I	Net Worth (Total Assets Less Total Liabilities)	I I
	I I		
TOTAL	I I	TOTAL	I I

ANNUAL INCOME	APPLICANT	CO-APPLICANT	CONTINGENT LIABILITIES	
Salary	I I	I I	As Endorser	I I
Commissions	I I	I I	As Guarantor	I I
Dividends	I I	I I	Lawsuits	I I
Interest	I I	I I	For Taxes	I I
Rentals	I I	I I	Other (Detail)	I I
Alimony, child support or maintenance (you need not show this unless you wish us to consider it).	I I	I I		I I
	I I	I I		I I
	I I	I I		I I
Other	I I	I I	☐ Check here if "None"	I I
	I I	I I		I I
TOTAL INCOME	I I	I I	TOTAL CONTINGENT LIABILITIES	I I

SCHEDULE 1 DUE FROM FRIENDS, RELATIVES & OTHERS

Name of Debtor	Owed To	Collateral	How Payable	Maturity Date	Unpaid Balance
			$ per		I I
			$ per		I I
			$ per		I I
				TOTAL	I I

SCHEDULE 2 MORTGAGE AND CONTRACTS FOR DEED OWNED

Name of Debtor	Type of Property	1st or 2nd Lien	Owed To	How Payable	Unpaid Balance
				$ per	I I
				$ per	I I
				$ per	I I
				$ per	I I
				TOTAL	I I

SCHEDULE 3 SECURITIES OWNED

No. Shares or Bond Amount	Description	In Whose Name(s) Registered	Cost	Present Market Value	L-listed U-unlisted
		TOTAL			

SCHEDULE 4 LIFE INSURANCE

Insured	Insurance Company	Beneficiary	Face Value of Policy	Cash Value	Loans
		TOTAL			

SCHEDULE 5 REAL ESTATE

Address and Type of Property	Title in Name(s) of	Monthly Income	Cost Year Acquired	Present Market Value	Amount of Insurance
Homestead			$_____ Year		
			$_____ Year		
			$_____ Year		
			$_____ Year		
			$_____ Year		

SCHEDULE 6 MORTGAGES OR LIENS ON REAL ESTATE

To Whom Payable	How Payable	Interest Rate	Maturity Date	Unpaid Balance
Homestead	$_____ per			
	$_____ per			
	$_____ per			
	$_____ per			
	$_____ per			

SCHEDULE 7 NOTES PAYABLE BANKS & OTHERS AND INSTALLMENT CONTRACTS PAYABLE

To Whom Payable	Address	Collateral or Unsecured	How Payable	Unpaid Balance
			$_____ per	
			$_____ per	
			$_____ per	
			$_____ per	
			$_____ per	
			$_____ per	
			$_____ per	
			$_____ per	

	APPLICANT	CO-APPLICANT
Have you ever gone through bankruptcy or had a judgment against you?	☐ Yes ☐ No	☐ Yes ☐ No
Are any assets pledged or debts secured except as shown?	☐ Yes ☐ No	☐ Yes ☐ No
Have you made a will?	☐ Yes ☐ No	☐ Yes ☐ No
Number of Dependents (If "None" check None)	_____ ☐ None	_____ ☐ None
Marital Status (answer only if this financial statement is provided in connection with a request for secured credit or applicant is seeking a joint account with spouse.)	☐ Married ☐ Separated ☐ Unmarried	☐ Married ☐ Separated ☐ Unmarried

(Unmarried includes single, divorced, widowed)

The foregoing statement, submitted for the purpose of obtaining credit, is true and correct in every detail and fairly shows my/our financial condition at the time indicated. I/we will give you prompt written notice of any subsequent substantial change in such financial condition occurring before discharge of my/our obligations to you. I/we understand that you will retain this personal financial statement whether or not you approve the credit in connection with which it is submitted. You are authorized to check my/our credit and employment history or any other information contained herein.

THE UNDERSIGNED CERTIFY THAT THE INFORMATION CONTAINED ON THIS FORM HAS BEEN CAREFULLY REVIEWED AND THAT IT IS TRUE AND CORRECT IN ALL RESPECTS.

_____   _____
Date   Your Signature

_____   _____
Date   Co-Applicant Signature (if you are requesting the financial accommodation jointly)

5

FINANCIAL MOMENTUM

*"Every man is enthusiastic at times.
One man has enthusiasm for thirty minutes —
another for thirty days, but it is the man who has it
for thirty years who makes a success in life."*
                                                    Edward B. Butler

FOR THE PURPOSE of our discussion we will define financial momentum as the financial mass times the rate of return. Financial mass is the amount of money available to earn interest. Rate of return is the historical interest rate earned on invested funds. When no historical interest rate is available, such as in just starting your financial journey, use the expected interest rate you might receive on your invested funds, and rest assured by next year you will have historical information. Financial momentum is measured as the value of the anticipated interest or growth available to assist you on your financial journey next year.

Now that we have examined the interest factor, are familiar with financial statements, and are developing an appreciation of the inherent forces constantly exerting themselves on our financial status from a more global perspective, we are in a position to appreciate financial momentum. What this means is that it is time to take a look at the net worth of the family financial unit and more specifically how this net worth is changing with time.

A key question to ask at this juncture is, if we keep doing what we have been doing, will our financial position (net worth) be greater next month than it is this month? Another way of stating the question might be, what are we doing this month to improve our financial position next month? Or, what financial currents are in place which are continuously effecting our financial progress?

From the 'moon perspective' (Chapter 10) it is possible to project where you are likely to be financially several years down the road of time by viewing where you are currently headed on a month to month basis. It's no big surprise to see the financially astute young couple who are working together to reach their mutual goals be among the financially independent 20 or 25 years later. On the other hand those who are making no monthly progress at their initial interview are most likely still in a 'hand to mouth,' 'month to month,' 'paycheck to paycheck' financial environment 25 years later. What do we learn from this?

The direction you choose to head on a month to month basis determines where you will be on the financial scale 10 or 25 or 30 years in the future. It's the little things, the small sacrifices which will allow greater contribution to investment funds or appreciating assets which lead to that wonderful place known as financial freedom. Or, it might be the extra effort put forth by the young individual or couple, (who, by the way, usually possess plenty of extra energy for such activities) who finds a profitable hobby or gets an extra job or two and disciplines to place the proceeds from the extra activities in a growth vehicle for future security.

The visualization of what life will be like in the future is of utmost importance. Regular contributions toward your future which are deposited in an interest bearing, or appreciating financial vehicle will grow to provide the where with all for a considerably more comfortable and enjoyable life. Having the 'picture goal' of where you are headed financially is a powerful motivator for keeping on keeping on when the going gets tough as, it surely will at times.

Your accumulated nest egg assets plus your regular contributions for the year, times your historical growth rate equals the momentum of your current financial plan. This is usually computed on an annual basis, but can be calculated at any time by simply plugging into the following formula.

FINANCIAL MOMENTUM FORMULA

[value of fund at end of last year +
(½)(12x current monthly contribution)] x
historical growth rate = financial momentum

The ½ factor is used as a rough estimation that on average the monthly contributions will receive interest for ½ year.

EXAMPLE:

If you had $20,000 in your savings fund at the end of last calendar year and are contributing $200 per month this year and have a historical growth rate of 12%, your financial momentum factor for the current year is:

[$20,000 + (½)(12)(200)] x .12 =

[$21,200] x .12 = $2,544

What this means is that by the end of the current year if contributions continue constant and if earnings are consistent with the historical past, earnings this year on accumulations made through this year will equal $2,544.

A nice aspect of the momentum factor is that it is a moving target and is ever increasing as this year's contributions will also experience earnings growth as well as increasing the principle balance of the fund. Just knowing that this year you will have a $2,544 advantage to start with is a tremendous motivating factor and a great way to start out the new year.

Projecting ahead a few years, or looking into a couple's status who started this program several years sooner, we might see the previous year's balance at $400,000, the contributions at $400 per month, and the historical earnings at 15% (it is typical for interest earned to increase as more funds are available to invest). Plugging the numbers into our equation we have:

EXAMPLE

[$400,000 + (½)(12)(400)] x .15 =

[$402,400] x .15 = $60,360

WOW! What a tailwind, over $60,000 per year from investments you've built up over the years.

From this point on the growth gets really exciting. As we know from the rule of 72, the 15% interest will double our principle in less than five years, and with steady contributions of $400 per month, let's look at the momentum factor of this couple five years hence:

The previous year's ending balance is $843,530. The current contribution is $400 per month, and the historical earnings are still 15%. Plugging into our equation we have:

EXAMPLE

[$843,530 + (½)(12x400)] x .15 =

[$845,930] x .15 = $126,889

Stop and imagine for a moment what life would be like with *over $125,000 coming in annually from your past investments!* Wouldn't life be sweet? Does that get the blood rushing? Now are you willing to put forth the extra effort to get the financial momentum started and working for you? The important aspect is to get started on a serious savings plan. If you don't start on your financial journey you can never arrive at your desired financial destination. Make the commitment to start your financial investment plan today, and take full advantage of what you now know about financial momentum. This can be the most important day of your financial destiny and one you will forever look back upon with much pride and pleasure.

Financial momentum can be a huge asset once you have the ball rolling in your favor. Just as a giant snowball grows while speeding down a steep incline, so your financial advantage increases as it gains momentum. The discipline of steady, consistent contributions is the driving force that heads you toward independent wealth.

FINANCIAL ACCUMULATION FORMULA

[value of fund at end of last year + (½) (12 x current monthly contribution)] x historical growth rate + value of fund at end of last year + this year's contribution

---

Another way of stating this is:

Financial momentum + beginning balance + this year's contribution.

Assume you had $20,000 in your fund at the beginning of the

year, and that you will contribute $200 per month the coming year and you have had a 12% growth rate in the past. This will define your financial accumulation. The following table will show you what this looks like for the next five years.

[$20,000+(½)(12 x $200)] x 12% = $2544+$20,000+$2400 = $24,944*

[$24,944+(½)(12 x $200)] x 12% = $3137+$24,944+$2400 = $30,481

[$30,481+(½)(12 x $200)] x 12% = $3802+$30,481+$2400 = $36,683

[$36,683+(½)(12 x $200)] x 12% = $4546+$36,683+$2400 = $43,629

[$43,629+(½)(12 x $200)] x 12% = $5379+$43,629+$2400 = $51,408

* Your authors are aware these figures are not exact, and are rounded to the nearest dollar, but are demonstrative for the concept being portrayed.

And now things are looking up; a raise came through and you are able to increase your monthly contribution to $300. You are more experienced in your investment selections resulting in a better interest rate of 15%. Do the math yourself; here is approximately what years 10 and 15 will look like:

Year 10:
[$109,236+(½)(12 x $300)] x 15% = $16,665+$109,236+$3600 = $129,491
Year 15:
[$245,805+(½)(12 x $300)] x 15% = $37,141+$245,805+$3600 = $286,545

Some people feel that only banks and financial institutions have sums of money of this magnitude. Fortunately you know better! And now you know how to get there from where you are.

Now you have examined the interest factor, you are familiar with personal financial statements, and are developing an appreciation of the forces constantly at work on your financial position, therefore you are better able to appreciate the changes occurring in your finances from a more global perspective. Take a look at how your net worth is changing with time. Key questions to ask yourself: — are you satisfied with your financial progress? If not, how can you enhance it?

It's an accumulation of the little things, the small sacrifices that allow greater contribution to investment funds or appreciating assets leading to that wonderful place known as financial freedom. As you know from the rule of 72, the 15% interest will double your principle in less than five years. Let's look at what another couple have accomplished; we'll call them Rick and Barbara.

Rick and Barbara are both dedicated sailors. They first met at a national competition for their class of boat; it was love at first sight. Rick is an Account Executive with an international corporation and Barbara is a Phys-Ed teacher in a secondary school. They married six months after they met and together developed a plan for their future.

They would start a family in five years, until then Barbara would keep on teaching. They will save Barbara's entire earnings each year and live on Rick's income alone. They will invest with an investment club that Rick has scrutinized for some time and found that the group of 11 people averaged better then 15% for the last several years. The "15%ers" as they called themselves were happy to finally make it an even dozen. Here is what the newlyweds' accomplished. Putting their savings together after a honeymoon in the Caribbean, they decided on the big goal of owning a charter yacht in 10 years and retire to a life of sailing. They were able to scrape up $35,000 to initiate their investment plan. Here is how the first year's plan worked out:

($35,000 + ½ Barbara's wage $27,430) x 15% = $ 7,307
$35,000 + $7,307 +$27,430 = $69,737

Year 2

($69,737 + ½ $27,430) x 15% = $12,518

$69,737 + $12,518 + $27,430 = $109,685

During the last part of the 2nd year they heard scuttlebutt about a couple retiring from a yacht club's youth sailing program — what a possibility for a second job for both of them. To do something they loved to do and get paid for it seemed to be too good to be true. With their experience, they were given the positions right away. Barbara was going to take over the girl's program on weekends and in the summer teach a morning and an afternoon class. Rick would take care of the boy's racing team on weekends and captain the team's efforts. Pay was not a great amount, $600 a month for the two happy sailors.

Look at their next year's savings:

Year 3

$109,685 + ½ ($27,430 + $600 x 12) x 15% = $19,050

$109,685 + $19,050 + $27,430 + $7,200 = $163,365

Year 4

$163,365 + ½ ($27,430 + $7,200) x 15% = $27,102

$163,365 + $27,102 + $27,430 + $7,200 = $225,097

Year 5

$225,097 + ½ ($27,430 + $7,200) x 15% = $36,362

$225,097 + $36,362 + $27,430 + $7,200 = $296,089

See what determination and a good plan is able to accomplish? Rick was promoted to District Manager and they are planning on a baby now. Barbara will stay home with the baby but will be able to keep the sailing job. Rick will be able to save $300 per month, $3,600 annually plus most of his year-end bonus, which should be about

$5,400. Their savings at the end of year ten will be $656,107:

$656,107 x 15% = $98,416 per year.

They are ready to go for that charter yacht and fulfill their dream.

Stop and imagine for a moment what life would be like with over $98,000 coming in annually from your past investments, in just 10 years. Wouldn't life be sweet? Does that get the blood rushing? Now are you willing to put forth the extra effort to get the financial momentum started and working for you? The important aspect is to get started on a serious savings plan. If you don't start on your financial journey, you can never arrive at your desired destination. Make the commitment to start your financial investment plan today, and take full advantage of what you now know about financial momentum. This can be the most important day of your financial destiny and one you will forever look back upon with much pride and pleasure.

THE PRUDENT LIFE

*"Unfortunately, many people aren't too smart
about attaining wealth. They want the good life,
naturally enough, but they concentrate on owning
things — like new cars and bigger TVs instead of
stock in companies that make the things they want.*
Louis Rukeyser's Wall Street

THE FIRST GENERATION millionaires who have acquired great
wealth in relatively short time periods have a strong tendency to live
well below their means. They often live in their modest, but comfortable house for many years, when others in their income range
move up to a larger and more extravagant house every few years. The
'prudent' buyer would never commit to a mortgage of more than
twice their annual income, no matter how convincing the sales pitch
of a real estate agent.

In addition, they tend to take vacations, drive cars, dress and eat
like those whose income is a third or a fourth their own. They realize that well-planned investments compound and allow financial
independence later, while money squandered is gone forever. This bit
of insight quickly separates the financially independent from the
larger group who struggles to pay their current bills. Remember how
Rick and Barbara planned and reached their goal.

By realizing early on that their expenditures do not need to parallel increasing incomes, they are free to utilize the divergent sums of money to catapult the accumulating nest egg. As discipline continues and funds snowball, it becomes obvious they are on the right track to financial freedom, therefore continuance is natural. Favorable results are the motivating factor which further perpetuates their behavior.

Contrasted with this group is a much larger segment of the population. These are the people who, in anticipation of an increasing income, start visualizing what purchases can be made with the expected increases. They imagine how much happier they will be after they have all of these new possessions. Typically these people's imaginations are running in a much higher gear than their increases in income. The net effect is that planned expenditures actually far exceed actual income, and even if the increased income does come to pass they manage to venture further into debt. How often have you heard friends or neighbors say, "Oh good, my raise came through. Now I can extend my credit and buy that (whatever it happened to be) I've always wanted"? And, of course, they did go further in debt to satisfy their ever-expanding desires.

Their belief is that they will be happier with more acquisitions. This is similar to a mirage down the road which disappears as one draws close. Once they make the longed for purchase, they are not a bit happier, but once again they are looking down the road at even more purchases they can hardly wait to make, which will surely make them finally content. This self-defeating direction is very common and often continues throughout entire lifetimes.

Back to the minority with the foresight to invest the increasing portions of their incomes. They appear to have a built-in immunity to the constant barrage of temptations, which their less savvy counterparts succumb to. What is the reason for this ability to refrain from overextended purchases? The jury is still out. Some of the factors, which are suspect and being investigated, are that this group has:

- The knowledge that spending more money is not what makes people happy.
- The realization that an increase in income may be temporary and therefore one should not shift one's lifestyle to reflect the increase, only to have to retrench again when things return to normal.
- Strong, urgent desires to establish an investment (savings) fund for the purpose of having money in case of emergency.
- A conservative upbringing, and/or personality that predisposes individuals to have sensible-spending lifestyles.
- Input from peers, financial consultants, relatives, associates, or company financial advisors, or others who encourage saving for the future.
- A working knowledge of compounding interest and its long term potential for accumulating wealth.
- The foresight to focus on preparing for early retirement or accomplishing set goals.
- An acute awareness of the various options that financial freedom allows in retirement years.

7

TEAM SPIRIT

*"At its core, team accountability is about the sincere promises
we make to ourselves and others, promises that underpin two
critical aspects of effective teams: commitment and trust."*
Jon R. Katzenbach and Douglas K. Smith

TO BE AN INDIVIDUAL financial powerhouse is one thing, however once matrimony is added to the equation, wealth building takes on a whole new dimension. Each individual will bring their own values and priorities with them to the altar. This is totally understandable and to be expected, as it is a very personal and individual value system developed over the years.

When the husband and wife team are not on the same page with regard to financial philosophy, goals, and strategies, they can make no significant progress toward their financial goals. We have all seen the sad state of affairs which develops when one spouse is very focused on saving and the other is equally focused on spending.

This reminds me of a time when my wife and I had moved to a home on Mission Bay, in San Diego. With little forethought we purchased a double racing scull so that we could enjoy the water. Imagine our surprise when we launched the boat and set out into the water. Instead of heading across the bay, we went in circles.

We hadn't realized that because I was stronger than my wife, we would run into this problem. What to do? We discussed selling the boat, for I couldn't handle this type of boat alone. Finally, it occurred to us that we could compromise. I would row easier and my wife would try harder. It took a while, but as with most tasks, when you persevere, you win and eventually we learned to go straight to our destination on the bay.

By working together we were able to enjoy the result of solving a problem that brought us the shared pleasure of what 'team spirit' can accomplish. We also learned that it is easier to row with the tide than against it.

You can have the same effect if your partner in a financial relationship is synchronized in both thought and action. So it is of great importance for both you and your partner to be totally in tune with your short, intermediate, and long-term goals. Only when you both know and agree on your direction and how you will get there, can you achieve your mutually agreed upon goals. (Take another look at chapter 5, Financial Momentum, and see how Rick and Barbara sat down and discussed various options and came up with their winning plan.)

A logical starting point is for each partner to read this book, discuss it thoroughly, then sit down to set some goals and a plan for attaining them. When each partner comes up with an independent preliminary plan for attaining those goals, it will often stimulate the other person's thinking. Next, schedule some time when you won't be disturbed and study the two individual plans together. Usually by incorporating the best parts of both plans, a couple is able to create a combined plan that is better than either of the individual parts. The beauty of this procedure is that when you both contribute to the combined plan you are much more likely to fully 'buy-into' the final plan of action. Unless you are both on the same page you will (financially) be going around in circles. Refer to chapter 11, Personal Budget. This will give you a good starting point in formulating a plan which makes sense to both of you.

Remember that development of the financial plan need not be done in a single sitting, and can usually be more successfully completed in several sessions. Also, once the major financial plan is developed, it is still not necessarily cast in stone. It is a good policy to review your plan annually to see if you are on track, or if adjustments are indicated. As finances are forever changing, you will undoubtedly want to make revisions periodically as you discover new ways of increasing your contributions to your future well being.

It is important that the two of you write down your agreed upon ideas of how to handle income increases, windfalls, bonuses, and lump sum opportunities, which are likely to arise at some time in your future. Also, you need to discuss and agree on what to do about unexpected financial events.

Should it be mutually agreeable for one of you to handle the financial affairs, this is fine. However, it is still important for you both to go through the preceding exercise, as it is mandatory that both understand the financial goals and philosophy even if only one partner actually handles the finances.

When one spouse leans toward thrift and the other toward casual spending, it is usually in the best interest of the team for the more frugal partner to accept the monetary responsibilities if the team is to reach financial independence. The other partner agrees to be on a budget. In this way the financial goals of the couple are being consistently met, and both partners have access to sufficient funds for personal monetary needs. Some people have a natural inclination to save their money and others seem to feel as if money will 'burn a hole in their pocket' if they don't get rid of it right away. There is nothing right or wrong, good or bad about these tendencies. It is merely one aspect of the person's personality. The key is for both parties to recognize and openly discuss their different ideas regarding money so that a workable solution can be developed together and carried out to financial success.

After all, it's the long-term financial accomplishments of the family unit that is the goal. Who does which tasks, or the specific individual roles, is not significant, as long as the mutually agreed upon goals are accomplished.

8

SAVING...
THE KEY TO WEALTH
ACCUMULATION

IT'S NOT HOW MUCH you earn, but how much you save that creates wealth. The earlier you start saving, the longer the savings have to grow, therefore the more time the interest factor is working in your favor prior to retirement. On the other hand, if you have been negligent for a long time, take the philosophy that it is never too late to start. Get aggressive and get saving. Some very late starters have gotten serious and made up for lost time. The ninth inning is not the best time to start saving, but if it's the best time you have, go for it!

A hundred dollars spent today on consumables is gone forever. However, if that hundred dollars were invested at 15% interest it would yield at the end of year:

1   $115
2   132
3   152
4   175
5   201

6	231
7	266
8	306
9	352
10	405
15	814
20	1637
25	3292
30	6621

If 15% sounds high, read some of the Warren Buffet biographies where he averaged well over 23% annually for his investors for many, many years. History shows over and over again that over the long haul, the stock market is the place to invest.

Now that we have a glimpse of the profound impact savings has on our wealth accumulation, let's look into a system for saving. Savings don't just happen; those who are successful savers plan their savings well in advance. In addition, these successful savers are an extremely disciplined group. This is reflected not only in financial matters, but also in many other areas of their lives.

Let's take a look at some systems for savings:

STRAIGHT PERCENT OF INCOME

This is probably the most prevalent and quite likely the most successful of the systems and as in all the systems, discipline is key. This is sometimes called the pay yourself first method. The percentage of savings vary greatly among those interviewed, from less than 10% to as much as 50% of regular earnings. Once the system is in place, it is important not to alter it in any negative way. Regular savings, even if not huge, grow splendidly with the aid of compounding interest, and when they are constantly added to over an extended period of time, the results are exhilarating.

When selecting a percentage to start saving, it is best not to get too ambitious, as the ability to stay with your commitment is of even greater importance than the percent selected. If the percent is too high to stick with, the whole program collapses. However, if one begins with a low percentage it can always be adjusted upward as one becomes more accustomed to living with the program. When your check arrives, it is important to make the distribution to your savings first, then address your remaining obligations with the balance of your funds.

BONUSES TO SAVINGS

Some companies pay bonuses. These may be weekly, biweekly, monthly, quarterly, or annually. They may be small or large or anywhere in between.

Those disciplined future financially elite who decide far in advance to allocate their anticipated bonuses to savings are obviously far better rewarded in the long term than those who 'blow' their bonuses on the whim of the moment (expendables). Since bonuses are above and beyond regular income, which the family unit is accustomed to providing for its routine expenses, they present a unique opportunity for applying bonuses to savings.

INCREASES IN PAY

This can apply whether it is an hourly raise, an increase in salary, an increase in commissions (either percentage or volume) or an increase in profitability of your own business. This is a time when the family unit is accustomed to living on the previous funds available and if it is possible to discipline yourself to spend only the previously budgeted amount and save the balance, the results can be awesome. This system might be called "sticking with the previous standard of living when the income increases." In this situation if the income doubles and the standard of living remains constant, savings could approach 50% of income. With this serious of a savings plan, wonderful things happen in a surprisingly short amount of time.

REFUNDS, REBATES, INHERITANCES

Any and all windfall type funds are a perfect opportunity to increase the investment account. The funds are not necessary for daily expenses and therefore can go right into savings. It is a great family rule that all unexpected money goes automatically into savings. This way no alternative thoughts creep in and the "gambling mentality" phenomenon is not at risk. Gambling mentality refers to the chronic gambler who finally hits the long overdue jackpot and squanders his "winnings" with little or no respect for the value of money. This 'easy come easy go' attitude is prevalent with gamblers as well as many who receive significant sums of money which suddenly appear and were not earned. All other factors equal, money earned through hard work is more likely respected and handled with care than money which "falls from the sky."

It may be difficult for some to believe, but unearned money is more often a curse than a blessing. A recent survey of huge lottery winners revealed that when interviewed 5 years after their 'lucky day,' 80% said they "wished they had not won the money" What does that tell us?

LUMP SUM TRANSACTIONS

These can be from many sources, the typical being the sale of real estate, your residence, perhaps which you have inhabited a number of years and have paid off the mortgage. You may be moving into a condominium which has favorable financing and you end up with an extra $212,000 cash; perfect investment fund fodder.

Or maybe you sold your vacation retreat in favor of the freedom that comes with visiting many various destinations. *Wow! Another $137,500.* It's very comforting to know ahead of time exactly where these funds go, DIRECTLY TO YOUR INVESTMENT PORTFOLIO!

Start a savings plan as soon as possible. If you are young and have your whole adult life ahead of you, now is the time to begin a regular savings plan. If you are not as young as you once were, now is the time to get very serious about a regular savings discipline. Regular, consistent savings patterns have a magical way of growing, and with the miraculous phenomenon of compounding, your nest egg grows faster than you might imagine.

This is because of two synergistic forces. One, the regularity of the contributions, and the second is the compounding effect on your investment portfolio. For instance, let's say you are very careful with your expenditures and you are able to tuck away $100 per week. If you say impossible, then consider a part time job in addition to your regular employment. The funds from this additional source are designated specifically for savings. There is always a way when the desire is strong enough. Many of the financially independent interviewed had three, four, or even five sources of income when they were very young, and many continually have several sources. Let's say you have found a way and are committed to putting away $100 per week. Let's also assume you are able to average 15% growth on your savings. This 15% admittedly sounds high and it is a little high at first, with limited funds, but for the astute investor, as you can become, and over the long haul it is not unreasonable. Our friend Warren Buffet has done much better over the long term.

Contributing $100 per week and earning 15% interest, your accumulating nest egg would be approximately:

At the end of year 1	. . . . . $5,590
2	 12,018
3	 19,411
4	 27,912
5	 37,689
6	 48,933
7	 61,863
8	 76,732
9	 93,832
10	 113,497
11	 136,112
12	 162,119
13	 192,027
14	 226,421
15	 265,974
16	 311,460
17	 363,769
18	 423,925
19	 493,104
20	 572,659
21	 664,148
22	 769,360
23	 890,354
24	. . 1,029,498

Wow! Over one million dollars in 24 years!

This example is illustrative of your financial status twenty-four years from today if you adopt the consistent, steady $100 per week savings strategy. Now that you see the results, are you willing to put forth the effort to save $100 a week? Surely you will figure out a way. Seeing the end result in the beginning is a powerful motivator. Contribute $100 weekly, invest sensibly for twenty-four years, either on your own if you feel capable and competent or with the assistance of a trustworthy financial consultant, average 15% for the term, and you are a millionaire. If you start when you are twenty years old, at age forty four you are a millionaire and still nineteen years away from the once magical sixty five retirement age.

The wonderful fact is that a million dollars at 15% interest yields $150,000 interest per year. This is $150,000 the astute, dedicated forty-four year old has at his disposal without touching the principle. The other option is to let the principle keep accumulating, as from this point onward the principle grows very rapidly. Even without adding to it, it will double in less than five years.

Now is it worth it? Is it worth the extra effort to earn and save an additional $100 per week? For some it is, for some it isn't. This is a question which can only be answered in your gut. You feel it or you don't. If the thought makes your blood rush, your heart skip a beat, the butterflies in your stomach violently crash into one another as your head feels euphorically light, you may be onto something you are able to follow through with. If you do, chances are excellent you will never regret it!

TAX DEFERRED SAVINGS PLANS

Tax deferred savings plans include a variety and ever changing group of plans which allow, (within certain often stringent guidelines) one to use pretax dollars to contribute to one's retirement. Since these are subject to change as often as the weather and subject to various specific rules and regulations, it is essential to consult with a professional to evaluate the current options. The theory is to use dollars which would otherwise be heavily taxed to fund retirement plans. These monies are invested and constantly added to within the existing limits of the plan. Via this strategy, one is able to increase the size of the total assets with the use of monies which would have been largely lost to tax burdens had the plan not been instituted. As observed from earlier examples, steady, long term contributions can accumulate to exciting sums with the phenomenon of compounding. The 'sooner the better' and 'it's never too late' are the rules for this game. This is one of the more important vehicles which leads to where you most assuredly want your financial journey to take you. See chapter 11 for more information on tax deferred savings plans.

9

TOP VALUE

THOSE INDIVIDUALS which end up on the top of the financial heap consistently tend to have one trait in common. They regularly, consistently, and unfailingly attempt to get top value for their expenditures. They seem to have a sixth sense for value, and if they are seeking a product with which they are unfamiliar, they research tirelessly until they are in a position to evaluate quality and price. Once the research is completed, action is swift and smooth, however expenditures seldom are made extemporaneously without prior research. Even seemingly small, what we might consider insignificant purchases are transacted with great care. In these trivial instances it may not necessarily be the money, but the principle that matters. It appears it is like a game where it is important to receive the best deal possible for the monies spent. They tend to be very vehement about "getting the most bang for the buck," a term heard over and over.

For instance, looking at vacation packages, some astute purchasers ended up with twice the vacation for half the price from the norm. This is a four fold increase in value for those who excel at sniffing out the great values. Please don't mistake anything said here. A low price is not a good deal when the product is inferior, in fact it is a terrible deal. But in the vacation business as in many other businesses, situations occasionally arise where it makes sense for management to offer some spectacular bargains which bring a little more money into the tills rather than having vacancies or in the case of merchandisers, unsold product. Having a nose for sniffing out these deals seems to be one of the ways the "haves" separate themselves from the "have nots."

Speaking of vacations, some gurus proclaim the way to reach your financial goals is by keeping your nose to the grindstone, and that means not being off on vacation to some exotic part of the world. This is hogwash! Well-planned, astutely-purchased vacations are not only highly recommended, but in many instances more like mandatory for those desiring to reach the financial top. "Why?" you say. Because it gives the vacationer a chance to back off and get a good look at his current situation. Some people have worked for several decades without taking a break, a break which might well have given them much insight as to a much more rewarding course to follow.

Often on vacation, when the mind is relieved from the continuous everyday pressures, one awakens with a solution or an idea which is the answer to an unsolved riddle of extremely long standing. It's almost certain these answers would not appear while strapped to the proverbial "grindstone."

So though at first glance it may appear inconsistent to be promoting expenditures for a consumable such as a vacation, there are strong extenuating circumstances which validate this suggestion.

Nothing could be much sadder than the story of the retiree who, after 30 or 40 years on the job, with his nose to the grindstone, finds it necessary to find a job to supplement his income in the retirement years, when he could have easily doubled or tripled his lifetime income had he only stood back and taken a good look at his activities and reevaluated them 10 or 15 or 20 years earlier.

The high accumulators are unique in their expenditures for minor items such as garden or household tools like a rake or a hammer. They tend to purchase high quality products at a significant discount. These tools are very meticulously cared for and kept for a lifetime. This contrasts to some of their peers who buy cheap tools at full price and lose or replace them many times during a lifetime. All the little factors which appear insignificant individually are collectively an important factor in the wealth building story. It is more a discipline, a lifestyle, a way of living which those successful at accumulating wealth adhere to. They are not necessarily frugal, yet they tend to make a higher percentage of their expenditures on appreciating assets rather than on items which vanish (consumables).

10

MOON WATCH

AS THE NOTED psychiatrist Len Fielding says, "When you are per-
plexed by a situation, pretend you are standing on the moon looking
down at the actors on this stage of life. One of the actors you are
observing is yourself. From this perspective you are more able to
escape the 'emotional involvement' element so it is more possible to
view the situation objectively." From this angle, solutions are often
so obvious you have to laugh at the fact that they ever were con-
strued as a problem. It is often our emotional entanglement which
causes the problem in the initial setting. When you are able to
detach, and from the "moon perspective" even rename the actors on
the stage if you choose, yourself included, the solutions are often
much more straightforward. This technique can be helpful for many
situations, work, family, intimate relationships, as well as casual
relationships.

This "moon perspective" as we lovingly call it is so consistently
beneficial it is recommended to take a mental trip to the moon reg-

ularly. Some report daily trips, some weekly, and others report taking a trip to the moon whenever a situation arises in which they determine a new perspective is likely to be beneficial.

From the "moon perspective" one observes all the characters on the stage, (the stage being one of our typical environments, be it work, recreation, social, or an intimate setting) as if one were watching a play on the stage. From this vantage point one is typically able to get a handle on what the various actors on the stage of life are likely feeling and therefore what they are thinking in the various scenes. By more fully understanding the interactions taking place and appreciating the other 'actors' perspectives, one is much better positioned for positive interaction.

For instance, if one were having a real challenge with one's secretary because she regularly was not getting the reports back in time to be reviewed prior to the final document preparation, one might take a 'trip to the moon' to observe the situation from the 'moon perspective.' By mentally standing on the moon looking down on one's environment, it becomes clear the previously labeled 'insufficient secretary' is so overwhelmed with six phone lines to answer, two other executives to type documents for, scheduling of all appointments for all three, and taking care of endless personal needs for two of the three. These include, but are not limited to, tracking down gifts during her 'lunch break' for the bosses daughter's birthday party, finding wrapping paper, wrapping gifts, picking up one of her bosses children after an orthodontist appointment when the mom was out of town, and on and on. From the moon one observes this overworked, underpaid secretary arriving 45 minutes earlier and leaving an hour later every day than originally agreed upon when she was hired. It becomes apparent she is a 'super woman' who deserves an immediate raise as well as a couple of helpers to keep pace with the ridiculous demands on her time.

On another trip to the moon you might discover the neighbor you have been disenchanted with for a long time is equally perturbed with you and for some very good reasons. Wow! What an eye opener.

Whenever a situation exists in which the solution evades you, take advantage of the opportunity to totally detach yourself from the scene by mentally going into orbit and viewing yourself and those around you which you are interacting with from the 'moon perspective.' Since this view allows one to see and feel all participants' vantage points, the likelihood of discovering the way out of the dilemma is vastly improved.

As human beings committed to our very own existence, far too often we view the situation with strong prejudice in favor of our desires or benefits. Once we are able to get beyond this prejudice, often a whole new realm of possibilities become available to us.

The 'moon perspective' is also extremely valuable for viewing into your financial future. For instance, it becomes crystal clear if one has no savings and is not contributing toward a retirement fund, that if this trend continues one will arrive at retirement age totally dependent on social security. Depending on one's age and the whims of the then current bureaucrats, social security will likely be in the vicinity of somewhere between bankrupt and valueless when your turn to collect presents. With this insight at a time when there is still an opportunity to rectify this worst of bad situations, one is able to devise a savings plan which will afford a comfortable or even perhaps a luxurious retirement.

Looking ahead in time from the advantage of the 'moon perspective' is tremendously valuable in many aspects of life. When a person is unsure how to handle an upcoming interaction, it is most beneficial to journey to the moon, view the actors objectively, and role play out the various positions one might take. It's not too difficult to realize that if the stance you choose is definite and confrontive, the actor or actors you address will likely respond in a confrontive manner. This will in turn tend to escalate your response and the spiral effect is in play in a negative direction. However, if you see yourself interacting from compassion and love and the other person or persons doing likewise, you are able to watch the actors on the stage of life play out their roles in a manner which demonstrates a positive spiral to a pleasant solution. What great insight to be able to 'role play' your potential stances prior to interacting in 'real life.'

Congratulations, the 'moon perspective' is a tool you can benefit from for the rest of your life. Make the most of it. It's okay to excuse yourself right in the middle of a tense interaction or negotiation and take a 'bathroom break' which allows opportunity to 'play out' various potential stances you might choose. With your goal in mind it becomes intuitive to see which of your potential responses is most likely to lead the conversation toward your desired outcome. Happy lunar travels.

11

PERSONAL BUDGET

"I expect to spend the rest of my life in the future, so I want to be reasonably sure what kind of future it is going to be. This is my reason for planning!"

Charles Kettering, Industrialist 1950

IN OUR WORLD of almost unlimited resources, daily choices have to be made. This is true with your personal finances as well as in your business. Should you buy a larger boat or replace the damaged fence; send your child to an Ivy-League school or the State University? Each expense either fills a need or a desire. Even business decisions are too often based on the same need versus desire without reference to a financial evaluation. In order to avoid pitfalls, you must ask yourself, "Is this action contributing anything to the profit picture?"

I challenge you to plan.

Start with a personal budget.

A personal budget is what most people don't have, but it is the first step toward getting your monetary affairs under control. When writing a business plan, a personal budget is essential to determine what amount of money you must take from the business to be somewhat comfortable. If you constantly worry about how to pay the mortgage and can never afford a theater ticket, you will not be able to give your best to your business.

There are young entrepreneurs ready to charge into business who will say, " I am going to cut down on everything — no vacation, no movies, no gifts, no dentist. I don't need much."

Let me suggest that this probably will not work for long. I do hope that you do not plan on going into business to see how austerely you can live. My idea is to make a better living and start to put some money away for your future.

A computer can be much help in analyzing your budgetary needs. Use the spreadsheet from Excel for Windows, or any other program that offers a spreadsheet. To get a feeling for what your budget will look like, list all of the amounts you spent last year. Get the bills out and be very realistic in analyzing your expenses. Don't overlook little things like gifts and the long weekend spent away with friends, or that short vacation.

Set up the spreadsheet with the following items in your left hand column:

Fixed Monthly Expenses:

Mortgage/Rent payment

Property Tax

Home Insurance

Utilities (Electric, Water etc.)

Living Expenses:

Groceries

Telephone

Transportation

Child Care

Medical & Dental

Clothing

Vacation

Entertainment

Gifts

Misc. Personal Exp.

Other Payments:

    Life Insurance

    Auto Insurance

    Medical Insurance

    Auto Loan

    Credit Cards

    Savings

Total Expenses:

The above list serves to stimulate your thinking. Once you have your categories defined you are ready to fill in the figures (from your checkbook and your bills) month by month across the spreadsheet. The totals should automatically appear. What will this do for you? It will give you a clear picture of what you spent last year and how you spent it. Remember, this is history, so don't criticize yourself for what you spent your funds on, just evaluate. Now you have a basis to set up your future budget. I would like to suggest that the last item "Savings" be removed and, instead, write in the first section (Fixed Monthly Expenses), add, "Our Future". This will include your monthly contributions along with your investments.

Set up your new budget by scrutinizing last year's figures. Where can you make adjustments? Not much in the Fixed Expense section unless refinancing your mortgage is a possibility. Groceries? — no, you'd better keep on eating. Telephone? — maybe, cut down on 'long distance' calls, use e-mail instead. You get the picture I'm sure. Each January one receives a detailed list from the credit card companies of all charges for the previous year. It is here where most of the impulse buying shows up. In this area there is often room for adjustment, and with each adjustment, you can allocate more funds to the 'Our Future' account.

Once you establish a realistic budget, live within its limits. It is easier than one thinks — you can be well on your way to that first million.

OUR FUTURE ACCOUNT:

If you don't do anything else, please start an IRA account now! You and your spouse, if you have one, can each invest up to $2,000 a year from earnings. This can be invested in stocks, bonds, mutual funds or certificates of deposits. This will reduce your federal income tax. Any bank or stock broker can supply you with forms to get you started. I use a well-known discount broker, and administer my IRA myself. There is no charge. I trade on-line and can use all of the research tools they have to offer. It's great! I love it.

Here are some descriptions of the Individual Retirement Account (IRA), Roth IRA and the 401(k) plan. Congress often makes minor changes to these plans, but as of now these are the current facts: IRA $3,000 annual tax free contribution per person from their earnings. It must be funded prior to April 15th (tax day USA) to be a valid deduction on the previous years tax return. You cannot withdraw any money (without a 10% penalty) until you are 59½ years old. Mandatory withdrawals must be made by April 1st of the year after you reach the age of 70½.

All accumulations of dividends and interests are tax free until you withdraw your funds. In most cases you will be in a lower tax bracket by that time. The amount you must withdraw at age 70½ is based on life expectancy as outlined by the IRS. It is a percentage of your IRA portfolio as of December 31st of the previous taxable year.

There are a number of exceptions on the penalty-on withdrawals prior to age 59½: 1) some college expenses; 2) should you become totally disabled; 3) $10,000 to buy a first home.

If you participate in a company pension plan, you may usually deduct the full amount of your IRA contribution, however it is dependent upon the amount of your annual income. This is often adjusted upward by the IRS. The person preparing your tax will have the latest facts.

Here is something for you to consider. You can make your contribution on January 2nd of the taxable year or wait until April 15th the following year (a period of some 15 months) and get your tax deduction. But when you decide, remember that delaying your contribution for 15 months means you are losing the complete tax deferred interest earned on that period's tax free money.

Example: $3,000 contributed for 25 years on January 2nd, instead of waiting until April 15 of the next year, will give you an extra $20,000 assuming you receive an average 10% interest.

With a Roth IRA, the first thing you must know — you pay taxes on your $3,000 contribution, now, instead of when you withdraw at age 70½. Income earned is not subject to federal or state tax as long as the money is used only for retirement. The income limits on Roth IRAs are higher, $150,000 for joint filers and $95,000 for single filers. Contributions phase out as your income rises. If you start withdrawing at age 59½, the money is now tax free, providing the account was open for at least five years. You are able to withdraw an amount up to your original contribution at any time without a penalty. You can also withdraw funds for college or $10,000 to buy a first home.

There is no requirement that you take out any distribution at age 70½. The primary consideration in choosing between the two plans is your tax obligation now and your best estimate for what your tax obligation will be in your retirement years, sometimes a hard call to make.

401(k) retirement plans are employer-sponsored plans and you have an option to participate. If you have such a plan where you work, JOIN IMMEDIATELY. You and the company can, together, contribute up to 25% of your net salary or $30,000, whichever is less. The deductions from your pay are done automatically via payroll. This way you are certain it gets done and you will find you can actually get by just fine on the remaining income. The pre-tax deduction on your income tax return increases each year and is very substantial, on the order of something like $10,000. All earnings on investments are tax deferred. You can start withdrawing at age 59½ and it becomes mandatory at age 70½ just like the IRA. You make your own investment decisions within a barometer set by the plan. If you change jobs you can roll over your 401(k) savings into an IRA account.

Most companies match part or all of your contributions. This is like getting a pay raise and since savings are made through payroll deductions, you never see or miss the money. You can borrow from the 401(k) funds under most plans, as long as you pay it back, however now that you are becoming one of the financial savvy, you are not even interested in borrowing, but instead remain focused on interest flowing toward you, that wonderful tailwind which makes your voyage so delightful.

12

INVESTMENT RESOURCES

*"It is a socialist idea that making profits is a vice.
I consider the real vice is making losses."*
Sir Winston Churchill

WHEN YOU START your portfolio, help is no further away than your trusted computer. Here you can research to any depth, a company or mutual fund that you are considering for your investments. Most programs are user-friendly and often free. Following is a partial list to get you started:

MUTUAL FUNDS:

www.morningstar.com - gives you insights from hundreds of funds. If you become a member, for $10 a month you get access to even more detailed research reports.

www.closed-endfunds.com - research available on more than 500 closed-end funds. A terrific education center with in-depth information on funds.

www.fundalarm.com - alerts you to funds possibly in trouble. The commentary is very blunt, and just another tool to consider.

www.idayo.com - allows you to customize the fund — screening for companies you are not comfortable owning, for example, environmental considerations.

www.ici.org - The Investment Company Institute has put together a great program geared to novices. It explains the benefits of dollar cost averaging and offers other useful advice for beginners.

www.smartmoney.com - A very comprehensive Java-powered analysis tool which lists 25 top and bottom funds in many categories.

ONLINE BROKERAGES:

All online broker customers have free research tools for mutual funds and stocks. Most have complete portfolio listing with real-time updates available. You list your investments or the broker automatically adds your buy or sell orders as they are executed to your portfolio. You can access your portfolio by using a secure code word any time 24 hours a day, 7 days a week. Here is a typical line of entry:

Symbol	Shares	Value	Price	Change	Cost	Gain/loss	G/L%
OXY	200	5,960.00	29.80	-0.01	4,204.94	1,755.06	+41.74

Many will offer you a portfolio evaluation based on your investment criteria and risk tolerance. The online brokers listed here are all well financed and offer lots of extra services beyond trading.

Charles Schwab - www.schwab.com - "My Research" report is a most valuable tool. A learning center has tutorials on funds, stocks and bonds. This is very user-friendly with fast execution of orders. You have extended trading hours, online banking, mortgages, bill paying and free checking.

Fidelity - www.powerstreet.com - uses a portfolio tool which helps to determine the right asset mix for your goals. Mostly mutual fund orientated as this is Fidelity's primary business.

Buy and Hold - www.buyandhold.com - a good broker for long term investors. Low commissions — something to consider.

Credit Suisse First Boston - www.csfbdirect.com - easy to navigate, with stock focus and technology conference webcasts. Great fixed income section.

E-Trade - www.etrade.com - easy to use but service sometimes suffers from high volume. You have extended trading hours, online banking, bill paying, mortgages and free checking.

National Discount Brokers - www.ndb.com - user-friendly, lots of news, tools and charts. They have a unique tool, "Stock Pulse" that lets you see trends in stock's bid-ask spread in real time. Good for measuring volatility.

Merrill Lynch Direct - www.mldirct.ml.com - outstanding global research, a very comprehensive site with lots of extra services. Probably one of the best organized sites. Well worth a try.

BONDS:

Smart Money - www.smartmoney.com - has an excellent primer on laddering a bond portfolio. (This is a technique to buy bonds that have different maturity and dividend dates.)

Bureau of the Public Debt Online - www.publicdebt.treas.gov - a clearinghouse for all types of government debts. You can buy treasury bonds directly at auction.

Investing in Bonds - www.investinginbonds.com - has great educational features for beginning bond traders.

Tradebonds - www.tradebonds.com - works like e-trade only for bonds. Catch — you need $25,000 minimum to start investing.

This represents only a small number of the many brokerages available to you. There are about 150 investment companies competing for your business. Be sure you check them out well before you trust them with your hard-earned money. Try them out and see which one feels comfortable to you. There are also plenty of very good brokers that don't offer online service. If that is your choice you still can use your computer for research.

This list is provided for your convenience to name a few websites that offer great opportunities for you to try. If you need a quick quote and a chart, go to www.finance.yahoo.com. Also, look at Microsoft Money 2001 www.microsoft.com/money and Quicken 2001 Deluxe www.intuit.com.

The broker I use is Charles Schwab. I have watched them evolve from an early discount broker to a very sophisticated on-line broker.

My portfolios are updated in real-time all day long. Trading is very simple and confirmation of my buy or sell orders is immediate — no hassle. "My Research", a terrific program available at a click of your mouse, offers a multitude of reports. An analysis of my portfolio, with an evaluation of each stock, gives me a chance to be on top of my investments. I have printed out 11 page reports including insider trading, potential risks, standing in peer group, company history, forecast on earnings, and I can go on and on. E-mail notices alert me if something drastic happens to one of my holdings that calls for immediate action. I am happy with the service.

There are many other on-line, as well as off-line brokers offering similar services. You must determine which services, policies and charges best suit your needs.

When you invest in the stock market you must remember that prices of stocks are not cast in stone, they are dynamic. Ups and downs are natural occurrences and greatly hyped-up by our media. Checking long range statistics you will find an overwhelming case for investing at least a substantial amount of your savings in the stock market. Take one of my portfolios. In the volatile period May 2001, when the averages were falling daily, some of my stocks went down, but some went up. The important fact for me is that from January 2, 2001 to December 2, 2001, I was up 12.18% in this portfolio.

By now you probably have your personal budget all set up and are eager to invest money in the "Our Future" account — your savings, remember? I would like to suggest that you read some publications that will give you current investment ideas. I subscribe to Barron's (1-800-822-7229, Ext.281). This is a very up-to-date weekly paper. I also get Bloomberg Personal Finance (1-888-432-5820) and Worth (1-800-777-1851). You may find these two monthly magazines very helpful in influencing your investment decisions. When you subscribe to Bloomberg you get access to considerable extra information, and you are able to list your portfolio. The prices of your portfolio are updated automatically, but you have to put in any changes of your holdings yourself.

If you are high on Tech Companies, try the Red Herring (www.red herring.com) an up-to-date monthly magazine. Go to a good news dealer and pick up a copy of various publications. You will find many more than I have listed. See what you like best before subscribing.

AAAI, the American Association of American Investors has over 170,000 members. AAAI will help whether you select stocks or mutual funds and are a beginning or experienced investor. Many of my friends say the $49 annual membership is a sound first investment.

They may be reached at 625 North Michigan Avenue, Chicago, IL 60611-3110, telephone 312-280-0710.

Once you've started, you will receive lots of mail from all kinds of individuals who will announce that they have a sure way to make you rich, if you'll only send them a check for $250.00 for a one year subscription to their newsletter.

I receive 6 to 8 of these each week. They all sound great, but I like to do my own thing, taking personal responsibility for my actions. Last week my wife received a letter telling her about a sure thing — to open a *Bank* in the Bahamas no less. All she had to do was make an appointment for a one-hour telephone consultation. This to be after she had sent a check for $1,000. I am not kidding, this is a true story. There are lots of sharks out there.

You may find some good ideas in books. Here are four of them by very successful people — a good idea to consider following in their footsteps:

— *Warren Buffett Master of the Market*, by Jay Steele.

— *Beating the Street*, by Peter Lynch with John Rothchild.

— *Winning on Wall Street*, by Martin Zweig.

— *24 Essential Lessons for Investment Success*, by William J. O'Neil.

There is a lot of information available. My last comment — find a Guru that you are comfortable with and stay with his suggestions or principles of investing for at least a couple of years. Then evaluate your results, and if you are not happy, try someone else.

Good luck, and happy investing for your future.

On the following page you will find some of the well-known brokerage houses and their telephone numbers.

BROKERAGE HOUSE	TELEPHONE
A. G. Edwards and Sons	314-955-3000
American Express Brokerage	800-297-7378
Ameritrade	800-669-3900
Bank of America Securities	800-227-4786
Bear Stearns and Co.	212-272-2000
Brown and Co. Securities	800-225-6707
Charles Schwab and Co.	800-435-4000
Chase Securities	800-245-8812
City Group	800-221-7065
Credit Suisse First Boston	212-325-2000
Dain Rauscher	800-765-3246
Deutsche Bank Securities	800-334-1898
Donaldson Lufkin & Jenrette	800-922-9004
Dreyfus Investment Service	800-243-7549
E*Trade Group	800-786-2575
Fidelity Brokerage	800-828-6680
Fleet Boston Robertson Stephens	800-288-7726
Goldman Sachs & Co.	800-323-5678
ING Barings	800-221-5855
Legg Mason	800-368-2558
Lehman Bros.	800-666-2388
Merrill Lynch & Co.	212-449-1000
Morgan Stanley Dean Witter	800-223-2440
Muriel Siebert & Co.	800-872-0444
National Discount Brokers	800-888-3999
Nuveen John & Co.	800-257-8787
Olde Discount	800-521-1111
Paine Webber Group	800-221-3260
Prudential Securities	212-214-1000
Quick & Reilly	800-672-7220
Robertson Stephens	800-288-7726
TD Waterhouse Group	800-835-0245
US Bank Corp. Piper Jaffray	800-333-6000
Vanguard Brokerage	800-992-8327

SECTION III

GOING INTO BUSINESS

13

WELCOME TO THE WORLD OF BUSINESS

"...213 of business owners consider themselves successful beyond even their own expectations, and — if given the chance to start all over again, fully 78% of the respondents said they would choose to be in the very same business they are in now."

Louis Harris poll of 2,000 businesses

DRS. STANLEY AND DANKO in their highly celebrated book *The Millionaire Next Door* reveal that about two-thirds of the current millionaires are self-employed and that many consider themselves entrepreneurs. In addition, we learn that a high percentage of these are in businesses they started themselves, and that about 80% of today's millionaires are first generation affluent.

Looking at the numbers, we see that less than 20% of the United States workers are self-employed, yet account for two-thirds of the millionaires. It stands to reason that since owning their own businesses has proven so successful for such a high percentage of those who have accumulated wealth in the past, it is likely to increase your own chance of becoming financially independent.

History tells us that there are many very successful entrepreneurs who have not had a college education. The father of our nation, George Washington, first comes to mind. In addition, we might recollect Thomas Edison, genius of technology, Henry Ford of automobile fame, Marshall Field for his department store empire, Mark Twain, writer extraordinaire and Madam C. J. Walker, the first American woman to make a million who came from the cotton fields of the south.

Modern successes without college degrees include: Colonel Sanders, America's chicken king and Ray Kroc, of McDonalds. Microsoft's Bill Gates dropped out of Harvard in his junior year, and Michael Dell, of Dell Computers, spent only one year at the University of Texas before leaving to start his corporation. The list could go on and on. All of the above had that 'burning desire' that is the great motivator observed consistently in the great success stories. They all had unwavering determination to follow through on their plans.

However, in today's super competitive world (particularly if you decide to stay in the corporate environment and climb the ladder of success) a college education is important. If you are thinking of starting a business in the sciences or professions, there is no question that you will need a thorough grounding in that discipline. Stanley and Danko quote the following statistics: about 80% of millionaires are college graduates, and many have earned advanced degrees. Since at last count only 38% of our population are college graduates, it is noteworthy how an education also increases the likelihood of financial success.

Due to the fact that the vast majority of successful entrepreneurs started their own businesses, let's direct our efforts toward the possibility of owning your own business. True, starting a business means taking risks, while having a job offers considerably more security. With the job, you know within certain limits what your check will look like at the end of the month and for some people this is such a high priority that giving up the job and starting your own business is prohibitive. To those people the extra effort to start a business on the side while holding down a regular job is always an alternative. Many folks before you have worked a lot of extra hours, so don't limit yourself to 40 hours a week. With this kind of dedication, new businesses have been started at the rate of only a few hours a week. This might be a good way to get the feel of the potential for your business venture without giving up your regular job.

For those who have their heart set on attaining a wealthy status, and to the risk takers who are willing to put forth the extra effort to achieve their worthwhile goals, starting your own business is a logical course of action. If you agree, may I be the first to congratulate you, for this is most likely one of the biggest and best financial decisions of your entire lifetime.

It is not inappropriate at this point to celebrate, as it is through decision making that millionaires are created. Feel free to join this elite group. You are always welcome, but you must be willing to pay the dues, which constitutes the initiative to "pull yourself up by the bootstraps" and put forth much hard work, going the extra mile or at times several miles to attain your all-consuming goal. It is amazing but true, that once you have made a commitment to yourself to take on and succeed in a worthwhile endeavor such as this, you instantly feel much better about yourself and the whole world around you. It is as if you already owned substantial stock in your future financial independence.

Paul J. Meyer states in his *Million Dollar Success Plan*, "Develop a dogged determination to follow through on your plan, regardless of obstacles, criticism or circumstances or what other people say, think or do." This feeling of ownership and success is exactly the power and momentum which can pull you right on through some of the difficult times that surely are ahead of you on your climb to the top. A wonderful journey lies ahead, but there are sure to be some very rough spots in the road. Remember, always, the journey is much more important than the destination. Enjoy the journey!

Understanding the potential rewards that are available to those who put forth the additional effort and creativity to start their own business is a constant motivator. The next step is to determine for what type of business you are best suited. The book titled *Do What You Love, The Money Will Follow* makes a valid point. By starting a business in a field you immensely enjoy, it is so much easier and natural to put forth the extreme effort to become super successful. When you are able to work and it doesn't appear to be work to you, you have found your niche. Congratulations!

In addition, it is mandatory that your enjoyment produces sufficient benefit to customers so that they are willing to purchase your product or service at a price that will make your venture profitable. If, even through creative thinking, there is no way that this business can become substantially profitable, then it is back to the drawing board until you do come up with a winning scenario. When you are able to visualize yourself profiting in an area you are ecstatic about, follow your dream.

If your first choice or thought doesn't mesh with economic reward, don't despair. The number of options for potential businesses is huge and growing rapidly in our expanding economy. Enjoy the search and keep in mind what you are and are not suited for.

A good way to determine what that business may be is to take a yellow pad, make a line down the center, and head one column 'what I like to do' and the other 'what I do not like to do'. This self-examination, forcing you to commit your thoughts to paper, is valuable and often surprising.

For example, if you love children, look over the day care potential, a private school for toddlers, children's clothing stores, toy stores, educational toy manufacturing, and any other child-related businesses.

If your interest is woodworking, pursue opportunities in this direction. If you strongly prefer working outdoors, investigate options in this area in a similar manner.

Once you have found an area that is of real interest to you, research it in earnest. Go to the library or the Internet and learn all you can about your potential business and if it has the capacity to become your path to financial success. Talk to those already in the field. Talk to those in related fields. For instance, say you are interested in starting a painting business. Talk to building contractors, drywall contractors, paint store owners, lumber yard owners, painting contractors, power spray paint equipment sales people, paint manufacturers, and on and on. Via this method, you are able to attain a well-rounded multi-based impression of your area of interest.

Perhaps you are thinking about going into the painting contracting business, when through your research you may discover that most new construction in your area is going to maintenance free exteriors, and established painting contractors are not able to keep their current crews busy. This is valuable information. Or you may learn just the opposite which is equally valuable.

Also watch for trends which can produce a good clue as to what related changes we can anticipate in the future. For example, (back to construction) maybe local architects are calling for much more ceramic tile, granite, and marble products and less carpeting or many other trends you can take advantage of. This information may tell you it is a poor time to go into the carpeting business, a great time to go into hard surface contracting.

Our society is continually changing in rhythms and cycles. Being ahead of the curve, as they say, is most helpful and thorough research can take you there. To be at the right place at the right time with the right information puts you one up on the competition.

In addition to traditional ideas, keep your eye open for the more nontraditional. This may be a business similar to one that is doing well in another part of the country, one that is not available in your locality. If this is what you discover, be careful to be sure there is a demand for such a service or product in your location. Sometimes there is a very good reason for the void, in which case it behooves you to discover it prior to investment rather than after you have committed your hard-earned cash.

Other opportunities often lie in niche businesses. Finding this type of business and filling the void can be extremely rewarding, and could include businesses serving other businesses. For example, perhaps a large homebuilder would like someone to contract to clean his new homes and ready them for sale. Or a concrete contractor would gladly pay a premium for an independent contractor to invest in a service to pump ready mix concrete to his hard to reach locations (you invest $100,000, I promise you $200,000 worth of business in the next 24 months) a possible win-win scenario.

Unusual businesses could include products or services that are related to local needs. This might be a demand for fishing bait related to your local fishermen's habits, chimney sweep service, firewood for the wood heat craze, lawn care service, condominium or home monitoring service when the owners are seasonally absent. The list goes on and on.

SUCCESS LEAVES CLUES

Careful observation of very successful businesses reveals that they do indeed leave clues. These clues, sometimes straightforward and obvious, may be subtle and challenging to decipher. They run all the way from the entrepreneur's personal enthusiasm to massive capital infusion, to leading edge technology and all of the possibilities in between. For the remainder of this book we will be looking in the direction of the clues generated by the very successful businesses. Hang on — it promises to be an exciting adventure.

BUSINESS STARTUPS

The starting of a business can be an exciting, exhilarating, eerie, elevating, ecstatic and emotional experience. It can also be dreadful, devastating, disheartening, disastrous and a real drudgery. Why? You may legitimately ask, "Are there such contrasting outcomes from business startups?" There are so many aspects to this discussion it could easily constitute its own volume and in its entirety is far beyond the scope of this book. However, we will explore some of the dominant factors encountered in starting a business.

A major reason for business failure is that the entrepreneur's dream was never converted into an actual business plan. This all-important exercise forces one to think through every aspect of a successful venture. We will go into great detail concerning the ins and outs of preparing a business plan in chapter 14.

STARTUP COSTS

Startup costs can kill you, and often they are directly related to early business failure. Some of the wonderful success stories have been what we might call 'pay your own way' or 'starting on a shoe-string' type startups. An example might be the welder who started building spiral stairways in his garage as a hobby, or the ceramist who started selling her wares at craft fairs. This type of startup finances growth of the "business" through money generated from sales. The argument surely can be made that this is an extremely slow and painful way to start a business. While this may be true, it seems that paying significant amounts of interest and principle on a sizable loan when the business is not paying its way would not exact-ly be a pleasant experience either.

The advantage of the basement, or garage, spare time startup is that from the beginning it is profit driven. It has its own safety check built right into its very own existence. If it is profitable as a hobby or part time job, it may be able to drive itself to full time or to the point of a large enterprise from its own profits.

In this scenario you have your "day job" to survive on, while the new venture is growing and getting the bugs out. Although it can be extremely exhausting, for those willing to put forth the extra effort necessary it has been proven to be a great way to start a business. Another favorable aspect is that the builder of this business is afford-ed a great "grass roots" knowledge of all aspects of the business.

When your business is entirely financed by its own profits, it's on a solid foundation and not likely to end in a deep, dark hole of debt. Although this may not be the best way to begin your business, it is one of the safest ways. The beauty of the garage or basement startup is that overhead is minimized, and overhead can eat your lunch!

When the time comes to move from the garage into a rented, leased, or purchased building with employees and payroll taxes and other inherent business expenses, move cautiously. Plan and project cash flows carefully, as it can be a critical time for the survival of your venture. Fun hobbies have the potential for turning into nightmare businesses if they are not well thought out prior to expansion. This is not saying, "don't grow out of your garage." The message is "grow with planning and caution when the opportunity is right for growth". Hobbies are seldom greatly profitable; businesses have the potential for huge profits when they are managed wisely. So go for it; just think your way through before you act. This means it is time to sit down and write your business plan and convert your dream into reality. See chapter 14.

OTHER OPTIONS FOR GOING INTO BUSINESS

BUY AN EXISTING BUSINESS

Buying an existing business certainly can be a viable option when you find the right situation. A good way to learn to recognize a great opportunity in an existing business is to look carefully and thoroughly at several dozen businesses in the field of your interest. Take your time, get to know the owners, and learn as much as possible from each one you meet. It is also advantageous if you are able to work in the type of business you are considering purchasing. All of the learning obtained prior to being the one whose responsibility it is to make the decisions will 'pay off in spades'. Get the financial statements from the business owners or the agent representing them. Crunch the numbers, and make any projections in line with the historical past. While you may be able to improve the numbers in the future, do not rely on it in your evaluation. You are much safer when you are able to make the venture work on the basis of actual past performance. Once you have zeroed in on a particular business which appears will work for you, insist upon confirming the histori-

125

cal numbers with past income tax returns from the sellers. You are usually safe with copies of recent income tax returns, as business owners typically do not pay taxes on unearned money. If the seller is not willing to share past income tax returns to confirm income claimed, then you are probably better off continuing your search elsewhere.

Only after closely scrutinizing many businesses in your field of interest are you in a position to recognize a great deal. When you eventually discover what constitutes a unique opportunity, then watch for the right situation, which is often the highly motivated seller. This may be the owner who has made more than enough money for retirement and is getting along in years. Or it may be the one who has tired of the business, or has recently received a sizable inheritance, or even won the lottery. Whatever the individual scenario, the business owner prefers to sell the business. Listen carefully to the owner's explanation of his situation. Does it make sense? It must make good sense and you must be very comfortable with the answers you get to the many questions you must ask prior to seriously considering buying the business.

LEARN TO NEGOTIATE

If it is actually the great deal as represented, and the seller truly believes it will allow you to reap handsome profits for your effort, then it stands to reason the seller might be willing to offer you great terms. What constitutes great terms, you ask? We would like to see a substantially smaller down payment than the average of other similar businesses examined. In addition, we would like to see the owner carry the note at an interest rate more favorable than the prevailing bank rates, and the payments stretched out over an extended time period with no prepayment penalties.

These elements are not only good business, but are also a sign that the seller truly believes in your ability to generate sufficient income to make the required payments. The fact that we ask to stretch out the payments is only a safety factor that allows minimal payments if unexpected tough times are encountered. The no pre-payment penalty is because it is strongly desired to pay the owner off as soon as possible and avoid additional interest payments as well as having the inherent peace of mind that comes from owning a debt free business. Just because we ask for all of these advantages, does not mean we have to have them. However, if you don't ask you will most likely not get these advantages. Depending on how great the business opportunity is, some concessions from this 'letter to Santa Claus' scenario will normally need to be made to consummate the transaction. A certain amount of give and take is inherent in deal making, but starting out asking for everything you desire will often get you at least a portion of your ideal results.

Once you have found what you feel may be the right deal, get to know the seller very well. Learn everything possible about them right down to the most minute detail. This includes their current desires, what their 'hot button' is, what their short term and long term goals are, and any information available from any other direction the conversation leads. Then discuss various scenarios that seem compatible with their goals. Custom fit an offer that is dyna-mite for you and is likely to be comfortable for the seller. A true win-win solution! For instance, the seller may initially be asking for $50,000 down, when actually $10,000 per year for five years would fit their needs just as well. Valuable information can be gathered from your conversations with them. Maybe the seller is fearful of missing the business and will offer to help you part time for the next two years without further compensation. Many unusual and beneficial opportunities often exist if you are able to sniff them out and create a deal that is also favorable for the seller.

In some cases the seller may prefer not to receive funds during the current year due to his tax situation. In this instance it may be possible to set up a payment arrangement where the business is capable of generating sufficient cash flow to pay its own way! If this is the case, once you have obtained control of the business you may find that your effort to extend the hours or service, or in some other way increase the profits, can afford you an opportunity to pay your business debt in full more rapidly than anticipated. The astute businessperson is always on the lookout for ways to increase profits. It may be increasing sales or cutting costs or a combination of both. But 'where there is a will there is a way' for the 'whatever it takes' entrepreneur.

The first step, which may be the hardest part, is to figure out what the seller really wants. Does he want the weight of the responsibility of the business off his shoulders so he can relax? Travel? Does he want the satisfaction of saying he sold his business for a sizeable amount? If so, if it is indeed worth, let's say, a million dollars or more, you might give him the satisfaction of buying it for that much money. However, negotiate for loose and lenient terms, allowing you to come in with little or no down payment and a very low interest rate that affords you an extremely large cash flow. So what if it takes you ten or even twenty years to pay for the business, so long as your cash flow provides you with a splendid income above and beyond your payments to the seller. In the long run this steady stream of income may be ideal for the seller during his retirement. Another win-win outcome.

Once you focus your efforts toward "how can I get the seller what she really wants" you are on a path more likely to lead to a successful transaction. Getting into the seller's mind is the key to tailoring an agreement to the sellers liking. You may ask, "how can I possibly get into the seller's mind, when a business broker represents the seller?" If that is the case, a business broker is just another opportunity to get into the seller's mind. Arrange to have lunch with the broker. Point out that you are a serious buyer. In a friendly environment attempt to find out what makes the seller tick. Determine what they are looking for out of the transaction. When the broker comes back with a statement like, "they want 'all cash,'" explore the seller's tax situation with the broker and ask if an all cash transaction is in the seller's best interest. Perhaps you will discover that the seller wants to spend the next ten years touring the forty-eight contiguous states. *Bonanza!* What would likely work is an amount of cash up front for a comfortable cushion, then quarterly payments sufficient to finance their travels, with a severe penalty if a payment is late or missed.

Only through trial and error can you discover what works. When an offer is rejected, a question like, "what changes would be necessary for you to seriously consider this offer?" or "what part of this offer needs adjusting for us to make a deal?" is likely to head you in the direction of consummation. All it takes is one yes to make a deal. If you receive fifteen or twenty no's on your way to zeroing in to where the 'yes' deal is, that's all right. After each 'no,' go to work to see how you can best custom tailor a new proposal that has most of the results you desire, and may work for the seller.

It is important to keep in mind that there are many factors which are not monetary in nature. Discover the non-monetary ingredient and pursue it. These non-monetary factors cover a wide range, from a particular seller's own personal idiosyncrasies all the way to their deepest beliefs. For example, take a look at Hank, our local neighborhood auto mechanic who decided to retire after nearly fifty years in the business. Hank came to this country with three cents in his pocket, no family or relatives and no vocation. He was always intrigued with mechanical things and loved automobiles. The first permanent job he landed was as a janitor at the local elementary school. He was grateful for this employment as it afforded him a comfortable living.

By chance, one day he helped a neighbor, Tony, who was having a problem with his car. Hank worked right on the street where the car was stalled. He effortlessly unclogged a fuel line and got Tony on his way. Not long afterwards another neighbor, Emanuel, who was a friend of Tony's, was ready to leave for the airport. He was scheduled to pick up his new boss, whom he had never met, as the gentleman had recently been promoted to regional manager of his district. Emanuel's car would not start. Emanuel called Hank in a panic. Hank fortunately was able to track down a loose wire in the primary electrical circuit and get Emanuel's car running. Now he could get to the airport on time and avoid the calamity of not showing up to meet his new boss. Hank being the good neighbor he was would not accept any compensation for his services. From this point onward Hank's fan club just snowballed until he was fixing neighborhood cars whenever he was not working at his regular job. Eventually, happy recipients of his services started tucking dollar bills into his pockets, even though he would insist they didn't owe him anything. Hank was just extremely grateful to be appreciated and accepted in the neighborhood and his income as a janitor was providing for his needs. In time, Hank rented an abandoned garage and started helping neighbors in earnest. Though keeping his regular job for a time, he seemed available most of the remaining hours each week. As might be expected, his auto repair business grew to become a successful and lucrative operation. The rapport he established with his customers, his appreciation of them, and the income they afforded him was far beyond his greatest expectations.

When Hank got to the point when he was thinking of retirement, his first consideration was for his loyal customers. Making sure that they were conscientiously served in the future became his primary concern. Therefore, to whom he sold his business was more important than the selling price or terms of the sale.

Having come from a marginal background, he was both appreciative and frugal in his business. He started saving for a 'rainy day' early on and as his savings grew he started investing in opportunities, other than a savings account. By the time retirement age arrived, Hank was in great shape financially. He would easily be classified a very successful small business owner.

This story has a happy ending. Hank had a natural inclination for mechanical things and learned by doing. In addition his memory was nearly faultless. Once he saw an automobile's malfunction and figured it out, he wouldn't forget the symptoms or the solution. In this way, over the years, he was able to improve his efficiency and therefore his service to his loyal customers.

The success of Hank's business was truly overwhelming. As the years swiftly passed by, the demands for his services were far greater than were his energies to serve his customers. Then one Tuesday in early November, a young man who went by the name of Chuck stopped in and announced to Hank that he would like to work with him. The sincerity and directness of Chuck struck Hank as he looked out from under the hood of a Cadillac he was servicing. He was silent and his memory went back to himself, when he was about Chuck's age and still employed as a janitor, fixing automobiles evenings and weekends. Hank looked him squarely in the eyes and replied, "O.K. let's try it out for a week or two." As it turned out, Chuck had just completed an auto mechanics program at the local vocational technical school and had a fairly good grasp of some of the less complex mechanical challenges. Also, he was eager and willing to learn from Hank and quickly caught on when Hank explained things.

The two worked together for ten months until Hank had concluded that Chuck would take very good care of his long term loyal customers. At that point Hank sat Chuck down and outlined the plan for Chuck's takeover of the business. This takeover consisted of an agreement whereby Hank would retire and Chuck would work for four years, during which time Hank and Chuck would split the monthly profits. At the end of the four-year period, Chuck would take over the ownership of the business, the building and all of the tools and equipment. For Chuck this would work out to be about a 40% increase in pay from his current hourly salary, plus the ownership of the entire business in four years. For Hank it represented significant additional income for the first four years of his retirement, but more importantly to him was the satisfaction of knowing his loyal customers would be well cared for. This transaction is an example of the importance non-financial factors can play in business transactions. Chuck was in the right place at the right time for sure. More importantly though, Chuck took full advantage of the situation by displaying his work ethic, willingness to learn, integrity, and sincere desire to be of service to their customers. In return for his efforts, he received a tremendous reward.

More often the situation is such that the purchasing entrepreneur needs to take the responsibility for structuring the deal and selling it to the owner of the business. Only by learning of the owner's personal situation, his plans and desires for the future, and his 'hot button' is it possible to put a deal together that suits the owners fancy. It sounds like a lot of effort, and it may be, but the rewards can be huge for the one who successfully puts together the win-win transaction.

Now, many years later, Hank has enjoyed a wonderful retirement, with much travel, including several trips back to his homeland. Chuck has earned and is enjoying similar rapport with Hank's former customers. From the way these customers are flocking into Chuck's garage, they are obviously also very happy with the service they are receiving.

Transactions where everyone wins are well worth the time put into creating them. So don't even consider giving up just because the going gets a little rough at times. Reward often is commensurate with effort put forth in creating the transaction. Little effort little reward, huge effort huge reward.

Identifying sellers 'hot buttons' can be extremely difficult at times or it can be as easy as falling into it as Chuck found out. Keep your eyes open and your ear to the ground and sooner or later clues are sure to surface.

THE FRANCHISE OPPORTUNITY

Franchisors have a history and a track record that tells the prospective franchisee considerable information about the company. Like any other business venture, it is imperative to learn as much as possible prior to climbing on board.

The major advantage of a franchise-type business is that the purchaser, the franchisee, receives considerable support from the franchisor. This includes, but is not limited to, trademark and/or logo rights, access to sources of financial backing, architectural design, marketing, operating procedures, management controls, advertising assistance, employee training, help with purchasing, and quality control.

On average, the franchise owner earns 20% more than the non-franchise business owner. Statistically, a franchise is also four and a half times more likely to succeed than any other form of business.

The down side of the franchise is loss of flexibility. This is due to the fact that with the franchise business comes often strict rules that must be adhered to. Also, the franchisee agrees to pay a monthly fee usually consisting of a percentage of monthly sales, which goes to the franchisor. Don't forget, there is always a sizable initial investment, called a franchise fee.

A favorable aspect of the franchise business is that in accordance with franchise law, much information is available to the purchaser prior to investing. The franchisor is able to outline the up front costs, the probable financial scenario for the first few months, how many months from startup to dipping the pen into the black ink, and many other questions which might be of vital interest. They are able to make some very close estimates based on demographics and assuming average management talents. If you are able to excel from average you might expect to surpass their estimates. Of course, if management falters, the opposite is also true.

While it appears that safety comes with franchise opportunities, and much money may be earned, the financial home runs are most often reserved for the entrepreneur who goes it alone and is not a franchisee. Franchisees are, with average or above management abil-

134

ity, very likely to get a base hit, maybe even a double, and occasionally a triple. Those great (storybook) successes you hear about are the risk takers who stuck their necks way out, beat the odds, and succeeded in starting their own businesses.

The advantage the new entrepreneurial startup would have is that he is in complete control. He can do whatever he thinks will benefit the business. This is also the disadvantage. The reason for this paradox is that the franchisor over the years has tried an astronomical number of different strategies, promotions, hours of service, and on and on and only allows the franchisee to do those which have been proven beneficial. The point is that some of the entrepreneurs' 'great looking ideas' actually turn out to be 'not so great' and his freedom to exercise these 'great looking ideas' may be very costly to him.

Perhaps what this suggests is, if you desire the assistance of a franchisor, are willing to work within their framework, and pay them a portion of your revenues, that's fine. With lots of hard work this can be quite profitable for you. On the other hand, if you feel strongly about being totally in charge and are very energetic, not too risk adverse, willing to put forth extraordinary effort, do your homework, seek consultants in areas where you lack specific expertise, then go ahead, buck the odds, and show the world you can do it on your own!

BUSINESS PLAN

*"The man who believes he needs help from no one,
quickly learns he has a fool for a partner"*
J. Cory Pierce "Raining Money Workbook"

A BUSINESS PLAN formalizes your dreams, your hopes and your ambitions. Writing one is a task well within the capabilities of every business owner or potential entrepreneur.

The question most often posed is, "Why write a business plan?" In an ever-shrinking world, our global economy is highly competitive. With the emergence of new market economies, this competition is becoming more intense. Any business not having a sound, detailed business plan is like a traveler without a road map in an unknown territory. Developing a business plan is a vital function if you start a new business, buy an existing business or buy a franchise. Mr. Pierce always says, "Failing to plan, is planning to fail".

Here are several compelling reasons for writing a business plan which serves to create your road map to success:

— Sooner or later every enterprise needs financing, either through a bank or from an investor. A detailed business plan is a prerequisite to obtain an interview from a bank, an investor, a venture capitalist, or often a relative

— For a new business venture to avoid costly errors

— For an established business seeking a joint-venture partner

— For an entrepreneur wishing to become licensed for technology transfer

— For an organization, to justify a new project as the result of research and development

— To sub-contract with a larger company

— For any company exploring the export or import market

— And finally when you wish to sell your business at a profit

What is this business plan? You may think of it as an inventory of your capability to establish and finance a business, in order to market it successfully and profitably. Can you sell the idea — first to yourself, secondly to a moneylender or venture capitalist? Try this even if you don't need any financial help right now. This may be a simplification of the process, but be assured that this is what it is all about. In this document you will prepare a word picture of your company. It will reflect a true image of what you have accomplished and what you hope to accomplish.

It is of the utmost importance that *you* write your own business plan. The reason for this is because only by personally creating it are you in the position to explain every word and every figure. Of course this sounds intimidating. There is nothing worse than sitting down with a pencil in hand and a blank piece of paper in front of you. You wonder what to say — how to start. This chapter is designed to help you complete your business plan painlessly.

You will see advertisements in business magazines offering computer software that will write a business plan for you. All you would need to do, they say, is fill in the blanks on your computer screen.

This is a canned program, and produces a canned impersonal business plan. It is not recommended because it will not be reflective of you and your unique business situation.

Before starting to write down your dreams and desires, stop a minute to think of what you hope to accomplish with this document. It is basically the 'why', the 'where' and the 'how' of your reason to go into business. If you are seeking financing to get started, you must consider the person who will make a decision based on what you write. Let us review the business plan from several points of view.

BANK FINANCING

Bankers, and most investors, will look for what I call the 3 C's: Character, Credit and Collateral. Remember that a bank is in business to lend money and make a profit for its shareholders. That profit is the interest you will pay to the bank. Banks are not in the business of losing money.

When a loan officer looks at 'Character', he wants to see:

— Your background and expertise

— Your personal commitment

— Your enthusiasm about your venture

— Your standing with your peers, and in the community

About 'Credit', he is interested in:

— How you pay your bills

— How you have paid your loans in the past, if any

— If the mortgage payments on your home are up to date, and its payment history

— How you will be able to repay the loan

— What is your cash flow, or your anticipated cash flow

For "Collateral', he will review:

— The hard assets you are able to pledge should you be

unable to meet your loan obligations. This is the last alternative as no investor or banker likes to repossess assets. They are not in business to sell used machinery, buildings or homes.

If you look for bank financing or not, it is prudent to put on your business suit, go down to the bank where you hold an account and introduce yourself to the manager. Tell him you are preparing a business plan and will bring it in when completed, and would appreciate his reviewing it. Ask him to introduce you to the senior loan officer, as you would like to set up a line of credit.

It is truly amazing how many business owners do not know the bankers to whom they entrust their money. Inviting the manager and the senior loan officer out for lunch is one of the best investments you can make. Use this occasion to get acquainted with them, share your enthusiasm about your business, and keep them abreast of your latest developments. Prepare a packet which includes a copy of your latest media promotions and your current profit and loss statement for his files. This way, you will never be strangers when financing is needed. Following this procedure will pay the dividend of having funds available when they are needed.

INVESTOR FINANCING

Investor Financing is different. Here, you are dealing with an individual or organization that primarily looks for the potential growth of your product or service. They are much more interested in *you* and your management team than a banker would be. Past performance is a secondary consideration. If it is the right deal, they will sometimes invest in a company that operates at a loss. Be aware that investors want a good part of your company and to be your partner. It is not uncommon that they seek controlling interest, put members on your board and help manage your affairs. Your entrepreneurial thrust will be curtailed. This can sometimes be a good idea for the less business-oriented, high-tech inventor.

JOINT VENTURE

You are seeking a partner, maybe in the Euro-community to open new markets, both here and abroad, and perhaps in one of the exciting markets emerging worldwide. A transfer of technology will benefit you both. When dealing with foreign partnerships, keep the following typical profile in mind when you write the business plan.

As your new partner most likely will have only a working knowledge of English, it is prudent to keep your writing easy to understand. He is often impatient and looks for straightforward answers in his business dealings. Instant profit is not his primary concern; he is more interested in the future potential of the venture. Do not assume that your way is the only correct way to conduct business. Flexibility will be your greatest virtue. In the United States we all have done rather well in business, thus the opportunities for hardworking, dedicated owners can be very rewarding. However, that is also true in most countries.

With this profile in mind, your writing must be very precise and to the point. Use short sentences packed with information. Emphasize the benefits to your prospective partner in the venture from his point of view. Keep in mind, you are selling your capabilities, your ability to produce, and you have researched the new market's potential. His fundamental question will be what's in it for my organization? Isn't this what you are asking yourself also?

NEW BUSINESS

A new business has special requirements. Joint venture or business expansion plans are based on the past accomplishments of the respective companies. You as a new business owner will need to do a lot more investigation, particularly in the following areas: startup costs, site location, market research, cash flow projections and profit potential.

If you need funding, you must keep in mind which one of the moneylenders you will approach; usually it will be your bank.

But, perhaps you are one of the lucky ones that do not need any outside financing. Believe me when I tell you that sooner or later, 99% of all entrepreneurs will need outside financing for a building, machinery, computer expansion, etc. The wrong time to apply for a loan is when you need money. You are far better off to cultivate your sources at least six months before the need arises. That is why we always had a line of credit, used it sparingly, paid it off rapidly and thereby established sound relations for future needs.

In addition, expect a close examination of the areas of your business plan where you discuss the following subjects:

1. Your understanding of the market
2. Your marketing plan
3. Your personal experience
4. Your proven management ability

In the financial section of the business plan it is suggested to prepare three versions of anticipated cash flow: pessimistic, realistic and optimistic. The pessimistic version must still show the ability to pay off the loan commitment.

Every business plan needs a nondisclosure agreement. It should state that the information provided is proprietary and is not to be disclosed, copied, or otherwise compromised. A good idea is to have a control number on each copy of the plan that you distribute, and keep a register of when and to whom they are given and when returned.

Following you will find the outline for the preparation of the business plan.

OUTLINE FOR THE PREPARATION OF A BUSINESS PLAN

Your business plan must include:

— What your business does

— How it will be done

— Who is going to do it

— Where it will be done

— Why it will be done

— How it is going to make a profit

What are the elements of a business plan—

— Executive Summary

— Business Description

— Products and Services

— Marketing and Sales

— Operating Requirements

— Financial Management

EXECUTIVE SUMMARY

This is the cover letter, which will sum up your goals and objectives. This and the index will be the last thing you write after all of the other elements are completed.

BUSINESS DESCRIPTION

Give a detailed description of the business:

Name, address, reason for location

Explain the type of business: wholesale, retail, manufacturing, distributor, service

Discuss the ownership and legal structure: Who is the owner, type of structure, sole proprietor, partnership, c corporation, s corporation

Review the skills and experience of all principles involved with a resumé of each principal including the following:

Fields of special competence, academic background (any honors), experience highlights in general and as related to present venture, personal information, family, organizations to which you belong.

PRODUCTS AND SERVICES

Explain in detail what your product is and how it relates to the present market:

Determine the current market size - projected need 5 to 10 years in the future, competitive products, cost advantages and other related items.

Show your knowledge of your competition and how you plan around them, and discuss your advantages.

MARKETING AND SALES

Marketing and Sales are the *core* of your business rationale:

— Identify the demand for your product or service

— How large is your market

— How will you be competitive

— What pricing and sales terms are you planning or using

— What are your advertising plans

— How will your product be delivered and marketed

— Opportunities for expansion: geographical

market share

additional products

OPERATING REQUIREMENTS

Describe the equipment, facilities and people necessary to generate your product and services. Are you a retailer in a mall? Will you need two shifts? Three shifts?

How will your product be produced and made available to potential customers? If you are a manufacturer, do you use direct sales, a jobber or wholesalers?

FINANCIAL MANAGEMENT

Here is where you demonstrate to *yourself* and to a bank, money lender or venture capital investor, the feasibility and viability of your venture. This is a most critical part of your business plan! You will establish vital schedules that will demonstrate the financial health of your present business and the soundness of future projections. If you are an established business you need the following:

1. Income statements and balance sheet for the last two years

2. Projected income statements for the next two years

3. Projected cash flow statements for the next 12 months

4. Income tax returns for the last three years

5. Break-even point analysis with a graph

6. The names of all the principals, their personal balance sheets and methods of compensation

7. "What if" statements to illustrate you have a good grasp of potential challenges. Spend some time developing positive statements that will clearly demonstrate alternative approaches to any negative situation which may develop

8. Important documents such as insurance data, lease or rent agreements, patents, copyrights and any issues pertinent to your business

Now you are ready for the all-important Executive Summary.

Keep this as short as possible — 1 to 2 pages. It must summarize the most important points of your plan and give an overview to the bank or investor. You must generate immediate interest and enthusiasm and send a clear message of your commitment to the success of your business venture.

After numbering the pages of your business plan, create a descriptive index placed as the second item in your plan. All this sounds like a big problem. Remember that problems are only opportunities dressed in work clothes.

AN INDEPTH ANALYSIS OF THE PRECEDING OUTLINE

COVER

Now that you've made a commitment to write your business plan, let's start at the beginning with the cover.

Keep it simple and business-like, but eye-catching. Select attractive type. If you have a logo, use it, for it adds an air of credibility and organization. An investor looks first for the clear, readable name of your organization. This should identify the type of business. "Smith and Company" does not say anything. "Smith and Company, Electrical Contractors," tells the story the way it should be told.

Show the name of the person to be contacted about the business plan. In most cases it will be you, but it might be a financial officer, or other designated member of your group. If it is another person, be sure to include their title. Give the contact person's telephone number, including area or country code. Print it big enough to be easy to read. If it becomes necessary to search the business plan for whom to contact and how to reach them, you may never hear from anyone.

The same goes for the complete address. Do not abbreviate it in any way. Give your fax number and e-mail address, if you have them.

Next, we go directly to writing the Business Description. You may ask what happens to the first item, "Summary." Well, we are proponents of writing the summary last, as it will pull the entire business plan together in capsule form.

Get a lined pad of paper and plan to write on every other line, leaving room for changes and additions. If you feel comfortable typing on your computer, double-space for easy editing. Expect to rewrite most of the plan. Nearly always, new ideas will spring up and replace old ones as you work your way through.

Be sure that you are accurate and can prove every line of your business plan.

BUSINESS DESCRIPTION

Remember that the essential ingredients in all successful Business Descriptions include:

SHORT HISTORY-LOCATION-TYPE OF BUSINESS

— Give a detailed outline of the history of your business. Tell when it was started, the people involved, where it is located and the reason for its location there and what you create, manufacture or the service you provide.

— Explain what type of business you are in, like wholesale or retail. Put into words why you chose this type of business. Maybe you have extensive experience in this field. Tell your story here.

OWNERSHIP AND LEGAL STRUCTURE

— Be very precise in explaining who the owner is and what the legal structure is. If you are a corporation, list the officers and/or incorporaters. If you are an S-Corporation, be sure you state it. You don't want a surprise later when someone reads your plan.

147

RESUMES OF EACH PRINCIPAL INVOLVED

— Remember that this is not an application for a position; you already have one. You are the owner, the president or chairman. Although you don't want to inflate yourself, neither is this the place for false modesty. Be straightforward and honest about your talents and experience.

The resume needs to show the following:

1. Fields of special competence. What makes you uniquely qualified to do your job, to run your business.

2. Your formal education, with the name of all schools and dates of graduation. List any honors and special interests, particularly if they relate to your job.

3. Experience highlights. What have you done to increase your knowledge to prepare you for your present position? List all the places where you've worked before you started your business. Use accurate names, locations, date you started, date you left, and how it helped you to grow.

4. List family members, and indicate your marital status and your children with their ages. List special memberships that complement your standing with your peers and community — trade associations, Chamber of Commerce, etc.

Following is an example of how Gondolier Shoe (a fictitious company) may have answered some of the previous questions. Study it and see if you could improve on their business description.

1. Our business was started in 1991 in Sarasota, Florida by Luigi and Benny Lombardi, who are well-trained in retail shoe marketing.

2. We are a closely-held corporation and our name, "Gondolier Shoes, Inc.," is a respected name.

3. Our business is a retail shoe store in a busy shopping mall. The mall is close to a major highway with a traffic count of more than 30,500 cars per day.

Did you find anything wrong with the example?

Didn't you think that Gondolier Shoes should have been more specific about their product, particularly since this is the business description section? Let's start the second sentence over.

We are a closely-held corporation. Our name is "Gondolier Shoes, Inc." We specialize in upscale imported ladies shoes and accessories. Our imports are primarily Italian high fashion in the upper price range.

Do you see how you set the tone for your business? This store is bound to attract many businesswomen. Can't you see them all trying on shoes?

Let us reemphasize — the questions and the examples following all sections are there to make you think and to get you started. They alone certainly are not sufficient for a business plan.

PRODUCTS AND SERVICES

When you describe the products and services to be detailed in this section, put yourself in your customer's place. Think about why they should choose to buy from you. You must have something different to offer people.

In our highly competitive world it is of the utmost importance that you have a descriptive, catchy name, or powerful brand recognition. Think Gateway for a minute. When they opened a computer store in our area, they put a very large black and white cow on the top of their building. The building was painted in the same motif. Inside they created a barnyard effect and all the sales and tech support people were dressed appropriately to fit into the theme. I still have to figure out what a cow has to do with a computer, except that mine often is as stubborn as a cow. Obviously you will never forget that Gateway store. When your neighbors received the big boxes with the familiar black and white pattern, you knew they invested in a new computer. That is brand and name recognition.

THE THREE ESSENTIALS ARE:

— A detailed description of your products and/or services. Take your product apart and describe it just as you would to a potential customer. Explain what it will do for them, how it will make life easier, and the main benefits of having it. Outline how it fits into the present market, then spell out your vision of the current and the future markets.

— Tell how your marketing organization works. Who designs the overall marketing plan, and what is your main thrust, local, state wide, national or international? How do you achieve your sales? Do you have your own sales people or do you use distributors?

— Describe your vision for your company five years from today. What will you have accomplished by then? What will your physical plant look like? What do your anticipated sales figures look like? How many employees? What will your production per employee numbers be at that time?

YOUR COMPETITION

Be sure that you demonstrate that you have researched your competition well. Explain how you plan around them. Discuss your strategies with respect to competitive pricing or creating a better value for the customer or providing superior service. It is important to point out your advantages over the rest of the field. The readers of your plan want to know that you are well prepared to meet your competition.

This is the way the Gondolier Shoe Company addressed some of the questions:

We are open Monday through Saturday from 10:00 am until 8:00 pm, closed Sundays and on major holidays. Our products consist of ladies shoes, matching handbags and accessories. Sebastino of Milan manufactures these products in Italy. We are purchasing our supplies through a New York wholesale house. Our average discount is 50%. By volume purchase, we can obtain a 55% discount.

We offer a service unique in our area. Our customers can select custom-made shoes and bags direct from the manufacturer. These may be obtained in any desired color and delivered within two weeks.

Our main competitor is a fashionable department store that features Italian leather products. Their prices tend to be lower than ours. However, we can offer better selection and service, and we take pride in this.

Did this write-up cover the essentials satisfactorily?

When we look at the first paragraph, some improvements are indicated. Let's give it a try:

We are open Monday through Saturday from 10:00 am until 8:00 pm. Our products consist of the finest handcrafted Italian leather. Each pair of our high fashion ladies shoes is complemented by a selection of exquisite leather bags, belts and accessories. These are manufactured in Italy by the House of Sebastino in Milan.

We import custom orders direct from the 'House of Fine Leather' of Florence, and purchase the complete line of the 'House of Sebastino' from a wholesale import company in New York City. The customary discount is 50% of the retail price. By annual volume purchase contracts we can obtain a 55% discount with 2% additional for payment within ten days. We take full advantage of both discounts. When you compare the two paragraphs, do you see the difference? Notice the emphasis placed on the 'high fashion shoes' and 'direct import of custom orders.' Remember, in your business plan you intend to *sell* your concept.

MARKETING AND SALES PLAN

Take a moment to turn to page 140 and review what a Marketing - Sales Plan should cover. As experienced marketing people, we recognize that this is the core of your business planning. This and the financial management section will be important factors in determining your success.

Let us refine "marketing strategy" versus "selling tactics". They are quite separate entities. Marketing defines all the essential elements involving the flow of goods or services from producer to consumer. This means the design of the service or product, its packaging, its pricing, distribution and the communication of these elements to the customer through advertising. To reach these conclusions, your marketing personnel will have done extensive research into your prospective customers' needs, wants and preferences. Your conclusions based on their work will verify the demand for your product or service and the attitude and buying trends of the consumer.

Once you have targeted your market, and established a marketing strategy, the selling takes over. Your sales representative contacts the customer, presents the product or services and persuades them to buy.

You must be very precise in stating the demand for your products or services. You must state the size of your projected current market and possibilities of expanding that market. Explain your pricing rationale, your advertising plans and your distribution methods.

As an entrepreneur, you will be very enthusiastic about your project and therefore have no trouble writing this part of the plan.

Here, as an example, is what the Gondoliers wrote:

Our customer is the professional and upwardly motivated businesswoman who demands exclusive clothing and accessories. A secondary market comes from the well-to-do winter tourists.

Luigi Lombardi, our owner, conducted a market survey. He relied on the comprehensive statistics from the Sarasota Chamber of Commerce and data from the U. S. Census report. The traffic count came from the Florida Department of Transportation. These figures were augmented by those compiled by the administration department of the mall. Based upon these findings, there is great demand for our product. In the past two years sales have proven this out.

Our pricing falls into the upper one-third of the market. Although slightly higher than department store prices, we justify this by the extensive collection of high-quality products we offer.

Smith, Cline and Associates of Tampa, Florida handle our advertising. We are in the yellow pages of the regional telephone book with a quarter-page advertisement. In the exclusive Sarasota Magazine, available in hotels and tourist bureaus, we run a half-page advertisement. Four times a year we have an after-season sale. This is very popular and is announced in local newspapers.

Gondolier Shoes, Inc., in an upscale mall, is strategically situated between two fine clothing stores. We have adopted an Italian motif. Our three salesmen are dressed impeccably to represent gondoliers and trained to extend European courtesy. One of our corporate officers is always present to supervise and assist special clients.

Don't you agree that the main points of this section have been well covered by Gondolier? In your final draft of this section, you may want to rearrange or use a different priority, but try to make it as thorough as the above write-up.

OPERATING REQUIREMENTS

The Operating Requirement section of your business plan must cover the facilities and equipment you need to run your business. It should also explain why your business is in a specific location. The following are subjects that you must address.

You should be easily accessible to your customers. This is of particular importance if you are in the retail trade.

If you are a manufacturer, are you in the center of your target market? Are you in a location where raw materials are readily available?

What employees are necessary to produce the profit you expect, and what are their functions?

How will you get your products or services to the customer?

What management is needed?

Give a brief analysis of projected or actual compensation.

What provisions have you made should you outgrow your present location?

We all tend to be optimistic in our forecasts. However, it is a prudent manager who also knows that he may have to cut back and take longer to reach his goals. There is nothing wrong with this if his focus remains on his overall plan.

The following example shows how our Gondolier Shoe, Inc. handled their operating requirements. Look at what they have written.

Gondolier Shoes, Inc., has a 2680 square foot store with a glass front, which gives great exposure to our merchandise. Double doors lead into our showroom. An imported model of a Venetian gondola greets you, serving as a display base for shoes, bags and accessories.

Armchairs in groups of three are distributed about the showroom to establish intimacy. Two private rooms are comfortably furnished for client consultations.

A small counter handles transactions and gift-wrap. The rear of the store is sectioned off for storage. Through a computerized system in this area, we can locate any requested item in seconds.

Our personnel consists of three salespeople, a cashier, an employee who restocks our storage area and gift wraps, and a runner who gets merchandise from stock as requested by the salesperson, as it is our policy that our staff never leaves a customer alone.

We are investigating a second location in the exclusive Armand Circle area.

Are you getting a good feel of how to go from a mind-jogging outline to a real world picture of your business?

Not many new enterprises will start on such an upscale level, as of course, Gondolier did not in its inception. However, regardless of the size or level of your proposed business, answers to these details will remain just as important.

FINANCIAL MANAGEMENT

Now, we are coming to the part of the business plan people find intimidating. You might not have a problem with arithmetic, but profit and loss statements and, in particular, cash flow projections, may seem shrouded in mystery. This is where people decide they'd better find an accountant. Not so for the new business. If you are starting a new business, it is essential that you can prepare your own financial statements. To explain every figure to a banker or investor, you must understand how you arrived at them.

We are mainly going to address accounting requirements for the new business, as an established business usually has accountants.

155

However, we also must caution the established business — do not neglect understanding your financial statements line by line. Please do not hide behind your accountant. It is you who are expected to know the financial position of your business. It is impossible to over stress this point. Time and again people radiate enthusiasm about their enterprises, then completely withdraw when one analyzes their financial affairs.

Every business, very large or very small, only takes in money and then pays it out, hoping that the pay-out is less than the take in, for then, presto, you have a profit. See how simple this is? Keep track of where the money comes from and "credit" your account. Know who is getting paid, and "debit" your account. In a very large business there may be thousands of accounts which need to be monitored, and computers do a great job of this. In a new, often small, beginning business, there may be only a dozen accounts. If so, a simple manual bookkeeping system is often a viable option. We suggest you keep the financial records yourself so that you will become very familiar with the amount of money which comes in and goes out every day of the month. You will see if your projections need to be fine-tuned. If this sounds beyond what you are capable of, think of taking a basic accounting class at your local community college or adult education center at your nearest high school. The time spent here will pay dividends throughout your business life.

For a new business, a quarterly statement from an accountant comes three months too late for effective corrections. This lack of knowledge is a main contributor to business failings all over the world. Dreamers often do not want to look at the cold facts of reality, while successful entrepreneurs have their finger on these details at all times.

As your business grows, an accountant, in house or one of the many good accounting firms, becomes an essential part of your business. They will be the ones to keep you out of trouble with the many tax demands dreamed up by our government officials. Always insist on a monthly profit and loss statement. Read it; compare it to the last months and last years to see how you are doing relative to the other statements. This seems elementary, but it is surprising how many people are too busy to check their own data.

We have found accounting firms very helpful in setting up our books and giving us guidelines to do our own bookkeeping — often without charge. They appreciate our asking for directions, for eventually as the business grows (and they take over) it makes their work easier.

Now, let's see what the new business has to prepare.

The new business owner has the hardest job when it comes to financial documents, as there is no record of previous years to lean on. Right here is where we separate the serious entrepreneur from the unrealistic dreamer.

At the end of this section, you will find a complete business plan by a young exchange student from Poland. We had the pleasure of working with her, and while this was written a few years ago, before she returned to her native country, it is as valid now as it was then. (The only changes are the names). It will give you a good picture of what this document is all about. Also included are some blank basic forms to stimulate your thinking when you start on your own project. It is strongly suggested that you use an accounting form at first, with a pencil and big eraser, as you will make a lot of changes. Once completed to your satisfaction, use your computer or have it typed to make it look professional. A long time ago, when preparing a business plan, we did all the accounting work in pen and ink. The banker was so taken in by our detailed work and knowledge of our finances, that she gave us a considerable loan.

In the financial analysis, you will determine if your venture makes sense. Is the profit really there? If you are now employed and have your life budgeted to the reliable weekly or monthly paycheck, will your new business support you the same way? Are you willing to do with less until you turn profitable? What will you live on if things don't turn out right away? These are vital questions that you should answer for your own sake, and for your own peace of mind.

It may not be realistic to think that you can hold a job on the side until the new business gets going. This is particularly important when you go from a proven hobby to a business for real profits. Rare indeed is the person who can serve two masters at the same time for any extended period. (Some may opt to keep their 'day job' while getting off the ground, but the time required to get the new business going is significantly increased.) In many cases, unless you are willing to sacrifice, maybe money, surely time, to give your new enterprise 110% of your attention, the odds of success go down pretty rapidly.

If you conscientiously write your business plan, then look at your financial analysis and find that things do not look as good as you thought they would, there's no shame in holding off until you find a better way to accomplish your project, or to search for some better alternative.

Some people take early retirement hoping to start their own business, without having the slightest idea of what it entails. They hope to open a restaurant or a little store in some nice place to live. The best advice to them is: "If you are in your own business, you have the privilege of working 24 hours a day to make a go of it."

STARTUP COSTS

To compile the startup costs, it is prudent to enter every possible item that you can anticipate you will need. Do not estimate costs. Find out the exact price of each item. Get three bids on everything and then choose the deal — not necessarily the cheapest — that will serve you best. Pick the one that will deliver precisely what you want and on time.

Let's take printing for example. You will need business cards, brochures, fliers, stationery, etc. designed and ready to go the day you open your business. You'll require invoices for your services plus all of the little things to make your business function, like telephones, electricity, pens, pencils, coffee maker, cups for your clients, etc. The list goes on and on. Picture yourself on opening day when the first customer walks in. What do you need to serve him?

When you have your itemized list correctly priced, total the column. Then add a 20% cushion. There will always be the unexpected increases in cost and the overlooked items.

When you have completed your startup costs, you are ready to calculate the financial analysis. This is where you spell out that amount of money you require, as you see it. The cash you intend on putting into the business, in most cases, should be at least 20% of the money you expect to borrow (in some areas, your required equity position may be much greater than 20%). This shows your commitment to your new venture.

List the funds available, including the loan, then list the proposed use of these funds. The startup costs and the financial analysis often require some detailed reports. In the sample, the proposal from the leasing company would be such a document. It comes right after the analysis as a supporting document.

PERSONAL BUDGET

Now is the time the extra effort you put forth in preparing your personal budget in chapter 11 comes to fruition. You will need a copy at this point in your business plan.

MONTHLY OPERATING BUDGET

Next, we are going to prepare a projected monthly operating budget for the new business. Some of the figures will already be known, while others you have to estimate after your investigations are complete. The amounts you come up with are going to be the basis of your Cash Flow Statement. They will constitute the first month of the twelve months you need to prepare. This is a critical part of your analysis and much thought is indicated in its preparation.

First, write down all expenses you anticipate and then put a value on them. What is your best estimate of your income for the first month?

If you are in retail or manufacturing, your income portion may look somewhat differently from that of Constanzina's service business (as shown at the end of this chapter). Here is an example if you are considering retail or manufacturing.

PROJECTED OPERATING BUDGET

New Business

Income:

Gross receipts $7,920.00

Less: Cost of goods sold

Opening inventory $15,000.00

This month's purchases 7,500.00

Supplies (boxes, etc.) 250.00

Less ending inventory 18,000.00

Total cost of goods sold $4,750.00

Gross Profit. $3,170.00

Expenses: etc.

This will be the same for all businesses.

CASH FLOW STATEMENT

Are you ready for the all-important cash flow projections for your first 12 months in business? You have a good start with the completion of your projected operating budget (which you will transfer to a big 12-column accounting form). Although it will take some time to write and add up all those columns, it is not as hard as it seems. You can also use a computer spreadsheet program to make the work a little easier. You will establish a good sense of what your finances are all about, when you anticipate your break-even point (which is where expenses and income are equal); a significant day for every entrepreneur.

You must estimate your gradual increase in sales and your often corresponding increase in expenses. Take Constanzine — if she gets really busy, as we are sure she will, perhaps a third employee must be added to the payroll. Higher telephone, mailing, and office supply costs all will reflect her good fortune. Keep in mind, as cash increases, so do expenses.

Look carefully at the example form. Note on top "Cash on Hand". That is the money you put into the business and the anticipated loan you expect to get, less, of course, startup costs. This is true for the established business as well. Notice there are separate totals for "cash receipts". This is what you took in each month, and "cash available", what is left of the original cash, plus your monthly receipts.

Next come your expenses, which are separately totaled. Finally, you subtract this total from your "cash available" that gives your actual cash position at the end of the month as "cash on hand." So it goes for 12 months. I hope you enjoy doing this. However, don't get carried away with your cash receipts predictions. Be realistic. Put down what you think you can achieve.

Many people figure their expenses first, then see what has to be sold to meet such expenses. This is not an altogether bad plan as long as your sales predictions don't get out of focus. Staying on the conservative side by using figures anybody can see as obtainable is prudent.

The established business builds on past performance with the addition of new capital, or the purchase of another business.

ANNUAL PROJECTED INCOME STATEMENT

After you have completed the cash flow statement, your next task is to cross-add everything and prepare an annual projected income statement. From these figures, everything will be accounted for except for cash on hand, which is not part of your income. But you already knew that, didn't you?

The last three items on the statement (loan payment, capital lease and owner's withdrawal) are not really part of the income statement. However, they are good to show here as they are most informative to the reader.

How are you doing so far?

Hopefully you show an obtainable profit, otherwise your business may need some fine-tuning. If you did your homework and your estimates are conservative, and your numbers are looking good, you have a great future. Being in business is a lot of work and it's also a lot of fun watching your ideas come to fruition.

Success in business takes commitment, persistence and a plan of action. Most of all it takes strong belief in yourself, plus the will and determination to succeed.

Now we come to the last form you must complete.

PRO FORMA BALANCE SHEET

The pro forma statement reflects the expected financial status after the assumptions made in your business plan materialize. You will need to list all of your business assets and liabilities as they reflect your startup costs. They are divided into the following:

ASSETS

Current assets: cash, accounts receivable and inventory items that represent immediate cash.

Fixed assets: furniture and fixtures, a building you own and vehicles owned by the business, etc.

Other assets: licenses, if any, prepaid rent or lease, investments such as retirement funds.

LIABILITIES

Current liabilities: (usually items that are payable within the current year.) That part of a loan due this year, accounts payable, taxes payable, etc.

Long-term liabilities: the balance of notes and/or lease agreements, other long-term commitments.

Assets and liabilities must balance. Up to this point they do not. Part of the liabilities is called "capital," which is your original investment. Another part is "retained earnings", representing the unknown amount needed to balance the balance sheet.

The two items you will see on the balance sheet called "appreciation" and "amortization" designate the amount your government tax collector allows you to deduct annually as an expense. In our tax code there is a published schedule for every possible item, and a corresponding life expectancy for that item. This then becomes the basis on which one calculates the depreciation and amortization. You can obtain this information from your local IRS office or on the Internet.

Construct your own balance sheet. It is a vital accounting record summarizing what you own (assets) and what you are liable for (liabilities).

When you have prepared all the accounting records, cash flow analysis through balance sheet, you deserve to be congratulated. You are well above the average entrepreneur's level. I predict that you will be very successful.

In addition:

1. Both new and established businesses must add to the financial section, a discussion of their projected break-even point.

2. All principals of each business must prepare a personal financial statement. Most banking institutions have their own form for such requirements. You would be wise to use the one available from the bank you propose dealing with, as they like to look at a familiar format. A universally acceptable document is provided at the end of chapter 4.

3. Briefly state who will process your accounting records and where they will be maintained.

Also, it is essential that you provide "what if" statements. This discusses what will happen to your business when the unexpected happens: if you are sick, maybe incapacitated. Of course you do not like to think about that, but it is of real concern to people who you are dealing with. Also, what happens if your electricity goes out in the middle of a major computer project, perhaps a payroll? What will you do if you can't get supplies because of a transportation strike? These are some of the questions it will behoove you to spell out.

SUMMARY

The summary is probably the most important part of your business plan. You must capture the interest of your audience in the first few lines. They must feel that this is an exciting, well-thought-out and profitable idea. If not, no one will read the proposal you've labored over. Here is where you 'sell' your idea and yourself.

Your opening statement must describe what the plan is all about. Then, in capsule form, state what your business plan encompasses so that the reader is eager to find out more. To see what we mean, take a look at Constanzina's business plan summary.

CONCLUSION

Isn't it satisfying to have completed your business plan?

Now, it is a good idea to take your finished plan to someone whose judgement you trust. Ask them to read it and comment before you put it together in final form. Think about their remarks. See if you want to incorporate them. You may have to do some rethinking, or at least be able to answer all questions that are raised. These are the very questions a lender will likely ask.

When you are sure your plan is the best you can do, have it duplicated and assembled to look professional. Remember that it represents you and your business. For comparison, look again at Constanzina's completed plan.

Throughout the life of your business, keep a copy of your business plan in the top drawer of your desk, and refer to it frequently. Measure your progress against your predictions. A business plan is a dynamic document that needs to be updated annually. It is a yard-stick of your thinking, your actions, and your success.

15
CONSTANZINA'S BUSINESS PLAN

Your International Headquarters A Business Home Away From Home

Business Plan

by
Constanzina Saprinsky
Siekieki R 59 #C
Siekieki-Warsaw, Poland
Tel. 66-477-78-34

Summary

As Poland opens its doors to foreign trade, a possible entrance to the European Community, there is a demand for office services. The foreign visitor wishing to conduct business usually requires a conference room, secretary and translation capability. To this end, I have devoted my market research. I propose "Your International Headquarters" as an attractive venture that provides these features.

My academic background includes an MBA from the University of Warsaw. The extended training I received in the United States gives me special knowledge into the requirements of this business.

I request a loan of $50,000 for start-up cost and working capital. The loan will be repaid in 60 months from earnings. I plan to contribute $11,000 from my personal funds to insure its success.

The following Business Plan spells out my program in detail. I am available for discussion at any time. I have everything in place to begin operations within a week of your favorable answer.

Prepared January 1993 by Constanzina Saprinsky
Telephone: 66-477-78-34

Index
Your International Headquarters

Business Description

Reasoning

To become a part of the international community, Poland must extend its foreign trade to all nations. To this endeavor, I will devote my projected new business, "Your International Headquarters." I plan to establish a consulting and secretarial office in Warsaw to serve foreign visitors who require office facilities.

After graduation in 1990 from the University of Warsaw with a degree in Business Administration, I spent the year of 1991 with the accounting firm of Wabash, Ross and Fields in Chicago, Illinois under an executive exchange program. There, I served as an intern and acting consultant on trade with former Eastern Block Nations.

Returning to Poland, I became aware of the need for facilities to serve the growing number of foreign business travelers to my country.

My offices will be modeled after the ones where I worked in Chicago. The excellent relations I established while in the United States should insure a flow of clients from the Chicago Industrial area. I hope to increase these numbers by having my advertising brochures available at the Chicago offices of Wabash, Ross and Fields.

Location

"Your International Headquarters" will be a sole proprietorship. Its proposed location, a suite on the fifth floor of the Warsaw Towers building, will have two offices and a conference room for visiting businessmen, as well as a communications room, and a staff office.

1

RESUME

Constanzina Saprinsky

I was born in Warsaw, Poland in 1967. Before entering high school, my father, a Foreign Commerce officer, was moved to Budapest, Hungary and stationed in the Polish Embassy. I became fluent in Hungarian during our four years residence. I am single and in excellent health.

Education:
    BA University of Warsaw 1988.
    MBA University of Warsaw 1990.

Fields of special competence:
    International Commerce.
    Language Fluency: Polish, English, Hungarian.
    Computer word processing and applications.

Experience Highlights:
    During my senior year in college, I free-lanced as a translator for businesses, channeled to me through contact with my father. I averaged $450 per month, which paid for my education.

    One year internship (1991) with the firm of Wabash, Ross and Fields, CPA in Chicago, Illinois, in the United States.

Special Memberships:
    Polish Foreign Travel Association
    Warsaw Chamber of Commerce
    Chicago Foreign Trade Board (part of the Chicago Chamber of Commerce.)
    Polish Olympic Fencing Association.

2

172

Products and Services

Services

"Your International Headquarters" will be your home office away from home. We will offer the visiting executive complete secretarial services including: word processing, translation, telephone answering, proposal preparation, FAX and copying facilities. There will be a conference room, as well as private office space for exclusive use of our clients.

One of my main contributions to this venture will be a consulting service to foreign organizations. This service will guide them through the often difficult government regulations of the former Eastern Block nations. I keep in close touch with these constantly changing conditions.

Competition

Competition in Warsaw, a city of 1.75 million people, now comes from three telephone-answering services and one secretarial service having word processing capability. At this time their workload is so great they are reluctant to take on new clients. We will be the only business center offering a comprehensive service in one location with a multi-language capability. A recent hotel of the Hilton chain has a business center available, mostly on a do-it-yourself basis. We do not believe they are a competitor for our service.

3

Marketing

Primary
Market

We have identified our primary market: the business person coming to Poland to seek a joint venture, establish, buy or service an existing business. Our market research shows us that in the last three years the flow of prospective customers has increased dramatically. The number of visitors registered with the Department of Industrial Development has doubled in just two years. They come from Germany, Great Britain, Japan and the United States. Having consulted at their embassies with trade attachés from these four countries, I have been assured that this trend will continue. In fact, inquiries received are increasing.

If we target only 25% of the 1992 figure, we would have a customer potential of 865 if concentrated only on the English speaking client. Our consulting and all-inclusive secretarial services will establish us as the Warsaw headquarters for foreign business interests.

Secondary
Market

Our secondary market, only now emerging, will be generated by the many new businesses being established in other European Eastern Block countries who seek overseas partners and/or funding. Our consulting and translation services will enhance this market.

Advertising

We have contracted with the Obrinsky and Ackerman advertising agency to design our

4

brochure. They will handle placement of small advertisements in export/import oriented magazines in the target countries. Our advertising folder will also be available to embassy trade attachés, Poland's Department of Industrial Development, as well as contacts established in the United States. A display advertisement will be in the Warsaw telephone directory when published.

Pricing   Our consulting service will be priced at an hourly rate. All other services will be charges by the job. Labor, material and time will be the criteria. As we have extensive experience in this area, we will quote prices plus or minus 10% before a job is started. We expect payment when the job is satisfactorily completed. We will accept cash, checks and Visa cards.

As a form of institutional advertising, we will be available to speak on the need for foreign trade to trade clubs, trade shows and chambers of commerce.

5

Operating Requirements

Physical
Space

The Warsaw Tower building is located in the heart of the Warsaw business district. I have the option of a five-year lease for a suite on the fifth floor. The space is divided into two areas separated by a reception entrance. One side consists of two private offices and a conference room, which I have set aside for client use. The other side will include my private office and a large room housing our FAX, copy machine, computer, telephone switchboard, supply storage and a long table. This will keep our working area away from that of the client's. The suite is carpeted, curtained and ready for occupancy.

I have a bid for furniture and equipment from an office supply company in Warsaw. They will supply all of my needs on a lease-purchase plan with payment over a five-year period. Upon execution of the lease, they require the first two and the last three months payments, totaling $4,229.17. The monthly payments are $845.83 with a buy-out at 10% or $3,500.00 at the end of the lease. (See equipment list, page 10).

I will manage the operation and draw a minimum salary until we are profitable. I will need two employees:

One receptionist/telephone operator

One secretary with office machine skills, including word processing.

6

What If?

I have in mind two girls who see the potential of my enterprise and are willing to start with a somewhat less than usual salary. My initial outlay for the employees would be $1,300 per month.

I am confident that we will be very successful. However, I have had an attorney look at both leases. He advises me that the office space could be sub-leased, all or in part, and the equipment returned with no more debt. I would forfeit only the last three payments.

7

177

Financial Analysis
Your International Headquarters

I am requesting a bank loan of $50,000.00 at 9.5% interest payable in 60 installments of $1,050.00 per month. From my personal savings, I will transfer $11,000.00 into a bank business account.

Funds Available:
From Bank $50,000.00
From Personal. 11,000.00
Total $61,000.00

Use of Funds
Start-up costs (see details) $20,653.40
Cash needed to break-even point. 6,653.49
(see Cash Flow Statement)
Working Capital 33,693.11
$61,000.00

This amount of working capital will give me the peace of mind to go forward without worrying about meeting payroll or paying my other fixed obligations.

8

Start-up Cost for Your International Headquarters
Warsaw, Poland

To initiate lease-purchase agreement for furniture
and equipment (please see attached
proposal from IOFSC, Inc.) $4,229.17
To initiate lease of office space at Warsaw Tower:
First and last 2 months of 5-year lease ($1,170.00 per
month including electricity and building maintenance.) . . 3,510.00
Telephone system with 4 lines: 2 client lines
through switchboard, 1 fax line, 1 private line to
owner's office, all inclusive of installation and deposit. . . . 850.00
Stationery and business cards 25lb bond (2,000). 785.00
Computer paper, 4-part invoice forms, misc. paper 478.00
Coffee machine and supplies 345.00
Misc. office supplies (paper clips, pens, pencils, etc.) 349.00
Legal expense:
    Attorney fees for licenses and government
    permits to operate business 480.00
Advertising: Preparation of a 3-color folder,
        art work and printing (3000). 3,480.00
        Advertisements in four papers
        in each of three countries. 767.00
Sign painted on door (gold foil). 65.00
2 four-drawer filing cabinets with hangers and
2 boxes each hanging folders and manila folders. 487.00
Overhead projector for conference room. 389.00
2 software packages for computer (Lotus 1-2-3
and Word Perfect). . . . . <u>997.00</u>

Total. $17,211.17

Add 20% for unexpected expenses . . . . <u>3,442.23</u>

Total start-up costs. $20,653.40

9

Furniture and Equipment Proposal for
Your International Headquarters
by
International Office Furniture & Supply Co., Inc.

3 Executive offices (each)
1 diplomatic desk and swivel chair
1 credenza
1 small round table
2 upholstered chairs
1 desk lamp
1 floor lamp
1 desk set (leather-edged blotter, pen set, ashtray)
@$3,500.00   Total $10,500.00

1 conference table with 8 arm chairs. 2,700.00
1 computer and laser printer 3,050.00
1 FAX machine 1,980.00
1 copy machine with sorting for 10 copies. 14,875.00
1 six-foot table 240.00
1 computer work station with secretarial chair 485.00
2 storage cabinets @ $260.00 . . . . 520.00
1 small table and 4 upholstered chairs
     for reception room 425.00
1 small desk and chair for receptionist 225.00
                                         $35,000.00

This quote is for a 5-year lease-purchase option, with five payments to cover the first 2 months and the last 3 months, to be
paid at the execution of lease. Monthly payments for the 3rd
through the 57th month will be $845.83. Buy-out option at the
end of lease at $3,500.00 (10% of original lease).

10

Personal Monthly Budget
for Constanzina Sabrinsky

Housing:

Mortgage Payments $342.00
Utilities. 59.00
Homeowners Insurance 15.00
Property Tax 96.00
Home Repairs 10.00

Total Housing $522.00

Living Expenses:

Groceries $160.00
Telephone. 31.00
Transportation 54.00
Clothing 45.00
Dental Expense 20.00
Vacation. 20.00
Entertainment 15.00
Gifts (Birthday, etc.) 10.00
Miscellaneous Expenses 15.00

Total Living Expenses. $370.00

Insurance Expenses

Medical Insurance $35.00
Car Insurance 18.00

Total Insurance $53.00

Total Monthly requirement: $945.00

11

181

Projected Monthly Operating Budget
Your International Headquarters

Projected Income First Month:
    Clients renting office space
    (10 Clients 3 days @ 195.00) . $1,950.00
    Secretarial Services 600.00
    Translation Service (2 Proposals) . . 450.00
    Consulting (10 hours) 350.00

Total projected income first month. $3,350.00

Expenses:
        Accounting $25.00
        Advertising 181.00
        Automobile Expense 15.00
        Building Lease 1,170.00
        Dues & Subscriptions 12.00
        Liability Insurance. 21.00
        Miscellaneous Expense 100.00
        Office Supplies 35.00
        Postage 20.00
        Salaries (except owner) 1,300.00
        Employee Benefits & Taxes. 130.00
        Telephone 75.00

Total projected expenses. $3,084.00

Less Owner's Withdrawal 945.00

First Month Projected Loss . . . . ($679.00)

12

Cash Flow Projection First 12 Month Operation of Our New Company

	1st Month	2nd Month	3rd Month	4th Month	5th Month	6th Month	7th Month	8th Month	9th Month	10th Month	11th Month	12th Month
Cash Received:												
Cash Sales	7920 -											
Collections from Acct. Receivable												
Total Cash	7920 -											
Cash Paid out:												
Merchandise Purchases	7500 -											
Supplies for Store	250 -											
Expenses:												
Accounting	50 -											
Advertising	50 -											
Automobile Exp.	30 -											
Building Lease	700 -											
Dues & Subscriptions	10 -											
Insurance Liability	15 -											
Insurance Life	50 -											
Insurance Medical	125 -											
Interest Exp	45 -											
Licenses & Fees	10 -											
Maintenance & Repairs	25 -											
Miscellaneous Exp.	25 -											
Supplies Office	35 -											
Postage	22 -											
Salaries	400 -											
Taxes, Payroll & Empl. Benefits	87 -											
Taxes Other	25 -											
Telephone	65 -											
Utilities	95 -											
Total Cash Paid out:	9751 -											
Owner's Withdrawal	1000 -											
Cash Position this month	(2831 -)											
Add Cash on Hand beginning of Month	10000 -											
TOTAL CASH AVAILABLE	7169 -											

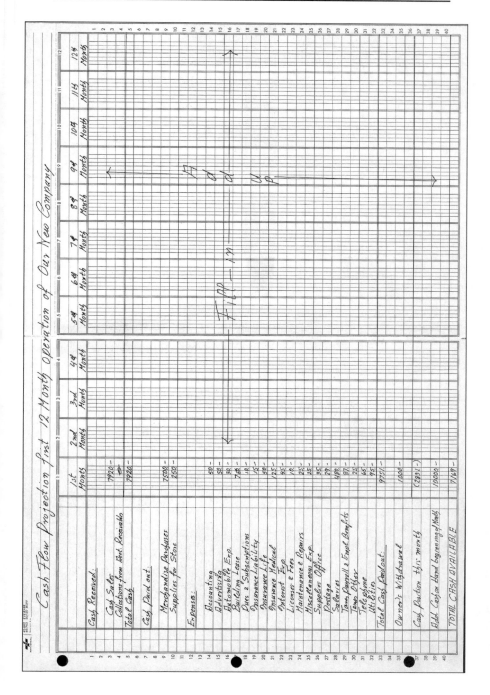

Your International Headquarters
Projected First Year Income Statement

Income:
Office space rental $25,875.00
Secretarial services 29,170.00
Translation services 10,795.00
Consulting 11,685.00

Total Income $77,525.00

Expenses:
Accounting $685.00
Advertising. 2,551.00
Automobile Expense 202.00
Building Lease. 14,040.00
Dues & Subscriptions 77.00
Insurance 252.00
Interest Expense 2,626.40
Miscellaneous. 1,700.00
Office Supplies 495.00
Postage 375.00
Salaries. 18,180.00
Employee Benefits & Taxes 1,818.00
Telephone. 990.00

Subtotal Expenses:. $43,991.40

Gross Profit: 33,533.60

Less:

Loan Payments 12,600.00

Capital Lease-Purchase. 5,831.90

Owners Withdrawal. 11,950.00

Net Profit: (before taxes). $3,151.70

14

Your International Headquarters
Pro Forma Balance Sheet
First Year Operation

Current Assets:
Cash in Bank Checking $13,498.30
Cash in Bank Savings 30,000.00

Fixed Assets:
Fixtures & Equipment 37,218.00
Less: Depreciation . . . . (4,316.86)
Misc. Startup Expenses 1,015.00
Less: Amortization . . . . (203.00)

Other Assets:
Government Licenses 380.00
Prepaid Rent 2,340.00
Prepaid Lease Purchase 1,749.57

Total Assets: $81,681.01

Current Liabilities:
Accrued Payroll Taxes. $1,020.00
Lease Purchase 6,998.28
Notes Payable 12,600.00

Long Term Liabilities:
Lease Purchase 21,003.44
Notes Payable 37,800.00

Total Liabilities. $79,421.72

Capital:
Owner's Investment $11,000.00
Retained Earnings . . . . (8,740.71)

Total Liabilities & Capital. $81,681.01

15

I am the sole proprietor, and will be reimbursed $945.00 per month at start-up. My detailed personal balance sheet is attached.

Break-Even Point

Our break-even point will be reached on or before the fifth month. My reason for confidence in this date is that currently I am preparing seven proposals for translation services. All were directed to me from our advertising company, who require translation of their advertising brochures. I am working on two now.

My attorney recently formed a joint venture with a German legal firm. For the past three months, I have worked for them in the capacity of business consultant at $35.00 per hour. Also, I have had a number of inquiries for temporary office facilities from my contacts in the United States. I am ready to go.

Accounting

All accounting will be done by in-house computer. An outside public accountant will review our accounts monthly. He will give me guidance at the start at no charge, and will prepare our tax forms at year-end.

What if?

I have given thought to what might happen should I for any reason be unavailable to manage my business. Consequently, I have searched for an associate to fill my role. I have been very fortunate to find an ambitious lady to be my secretary. She will sit in on my consultations to learn that part of our business. She is well

16

qualified in other areas, having recently left the international section of the Commerce Department, due to an economic move by the government.

Our computer configuration is identical to that employed by our accounting firm. In that manner, we will always have a back-up. I now use that system during their off-hours.

From time to time the telephone lines go out, meaning we would be unable to FAX information to clients in the United States. Fortunately, UPS has an overnight service to the United States, and to other countries. We can use their facilities in an emergency.

Attached is a copy of my personal balance sheet, my lease, business license and insurance proposals.

17

Assets:		Liabilities	
Apartment	.....$62,000.	Mortgage .....$32,000.	
1992 Toyota	...16,000.		
Furniture	......6,500.		
Cash in Bank	...12,480.		
Total Assets	.$96,980	Liabilities .....$32,000.	

Income:		Other Liabilities:	
Wages	......$15,240.	Insurance ....$816.	
Interest	.........748.	1993 Property Tax 1,152.	
		1992 Income Tax .1,478.	
		Euro Card ....250.	
Total Assets	...$112,968.	Liabilities $35,696	

Net Worth $77,272

Investments:

Real Estate - Four room, one-bath apartment.
Mortgage of $32,000 at 10.5% payable in
15 years at $342 per month.

	Initials	Date
Prepared By		
Approved By		

CAMBRIDGE
58242

Personal Monthly Budget for Constanzina Sabrinsky	Expenses	Totals
Housing:		
Mortgage Payments	342 —	
Utilities	59 —	
Homeowners Insurance	15 —	
Property Tax	96 —	
Home repairs	10 —	
Total Housing		522 —
Living Expenses:		
Groceries	160 —	
Telephone	31 —	
Transportation	54 —	
Clothing	45 —	
Dental Expense	20 —	
Vacation	20 —	
Entertainment	15 —	
Gifts (Birthdays-Christmas)	10 —	
Miscellaneous Expenses	15 —	
Total Living Expenses		370 —
Insurance Expenses:		
Medical Ins.	35 —	
Car Ins.	18 —	
Total Insurance		53 —
Total Monthly requirement		945 —

189

CAMBRIDGE
58242

Projected Monthly Operating Budget

Prepared By

Approved By

	Income	Expenses	Totals
Income first Month:			
Gross Receipts			
Less: Cost of Goods Sold			
Opening Inventory			
This Month Purchases			
Supplies Purchased			
Less Ending Inventory			
Total Cost of Goods Sold:			
Gross Profit:			
Expenses:			
Accounting			
Advertising			
Automobile Exp.			
Building Lease / Rent			
Dues 2 Subscriptions			
Insurance Liability			
Insurance Medical			
Insurance Life			
Interest Exp.			
Licenses 2 Fees			
Maintenance & Repairs			
Miscellaneous Exp.			
Office Supplies			
Postage			
Salaries			
Taxes Payroll 2 Benefits			
Taxes Other			
Telephone			
Utilities			
Total Expenses:			
Less: Owners Withdrawal			
Net Profit or Loss			

Your Cash Flow Projection
First 12 Month Operation

	1st Month	2nd Month	3rd Month	4th Month	5th Month	6th Month	7th Month	8th Month	9th Month	10th Month	11th Month	12th Month
Cash on Hand												
Cash Receipts:												
Less: Cost of Goods Sold												
Opening Inventory												
This Month Purchases												
Supplies Purchased												
Less: Ending Inventory												
Net Cash Receipts:												
Total Cash Available:												
Cash Paid Out:												
Accounting												
Advertising												
Automobile Exp.												
Building Lease/Rent												
Dues & Subscriptions												
Insurance Liability												
Insurance Medical												
Insurance Life												
Interest Exp.												
Licenses & Fees												
Maintenance & Repairs												
Miscellaneous Exp.												
Office Supplies												
Postage												
Salaries												
Taxes Payroll & Benefits												
Taxes Other												
Telephone												
Utilities												
Subtotal Expenses:												
Loan Principal Payments												
Capital Lease-Purchase												
Owners Withdrawal												
Total Cash Paid Out:												
Cash Position End of Month												
Profit or Loss												

CAMBRIDGE
58242

Pro Forma Balance Sheet

Prepared By
Approved By

	Assets	Liabilities Capital	
Current Assets:			
Cash in Bank			
Cash on Hand			
Accounts Receivable			
Inventory			
Fixed Assets:			
Real Estate			
Fixtures & Equipment			
Vehicles			
Misc. Start-up			
Less: Depreciation & Amortization			
Other Assets:			
License			
Prepaid Rent			
Prepaid Lease			
Goodwill			
Total Assets:			
Current Liabilities:			
Notes payable (due within 1 year)			
Accounts payable			
Lease payable			
Accrued Taxes			
Accrued Payroll Taxes			
Accrued Expenses			
Long Term Liabilities:			
Notes payable			
Lease payable			
Other			
Total Liabilities:			
Capital:			
Owner's Investment			
Retained Earnings			
Total Liabilities & Capital:			

TIPS FOR BUSINESS SUCCESS

*"To my mind the best investment a young man
starting out in business could possibly make is
to give all his time, all his energies to work, just
plain, hard work."*

Charles M. Schwab

NOW THAT YOU have completed your business plan and are ready to start on that exciting journey, here are some tips that have worked well for us and many other successful business people.

To paraphrase President Kennedy, *ask not how can I make more money — ask how might I better serve the needs of the community*.

The great business leaders all focused on a worthwhile goal that will benefit either many people in some significant way or some people in a dramatic way. We will endeavor in this chapter to explore many ways that may give you ideas to enhance your business. Since each business is unique as well as constantly changing, there is no one best solution for all situations. Some ideas work for one and not the other, some are good in one location but fall flat in the next application.

Typically business people who maximize their customer relations and constantly build on providing the most benefit to their customers will achieve overwhelming success. To them the customers are kings and queens. They listen to what makes them tick and capitalize on fulfilling their needs. The major difference between the wealthy businessman and the one just getting by is that the successful one is providing more benefit to more people. In the next paragraph we will take you to the moon and back again, so get ready to take off.

Owning your own business may be the beginning of your wealth building journey. Research shows the vast majority of the first generation financially independent created their wealth from cash generated by the businesses they own. To generate more cash flow will be your primary objective as you embark on your new venture. We are sure by now you have analyzed many avenues in which your new funds may be invested, as they become available. It is easy to get bogged down in the day to day grind and lose track of the direction the business is really headed. The noted psychiatrist, Len Fielding, suggested in a recent address, "Pretend for a moment you are standing on the moon looking down on all these people, you included, and watch them for a while, observe what they are doing. How could they be more efficient, more effective, and more productive? Later you may implement some of those ideas, which were so obvious from your *moon perspective*." By standing back and seeing the "whole picture" from a distance, one can often see opportunities available but not implemented. That is what Dr. Fielding is talking about and if it helps you to detach yourself by looking down from the moon, go for it. See chapter 10, Moon Watch, for more details.

It is essential that you make frequent assessments of your business and here is an item that may need to be evaluated:

DELEGATION

What am I spending my time on that could instead be delegated to an associate?

Let's assume you have a candle-making business, and you are pouring wax into the molds. You may very well be far ahead to hire a minimum wage associate to pour wax, allowing you to pursue new accounts or innovative new candle designs, or special promotions.

This candle-making example was chosen purposefully, for recently we have witnessed a small neighborhood mom and pop candle manufacturing operation explode into a multimillion-dollar business in what seemed like only moments. This candle-making model will be referred to on several occasions, as it is a great teaching tool on growth management.

From top executives of large companies, to the individual starting a business in the basement or garage, a glimpse from the moon may help prioritize the way the individual utilizes their earthly time on a daily basis. Whenever you see yourself involved in a task that could be accomplished as well by an associate with more time, delegation may make good sense. Once this time constraint is withdrawn from your schedule, you may be able to use your newly acquired time to allocate more effort toward guidance, leadership, and planning, which will likely pay significant dividends in the future.

My previous background included clinical dentistry as well as business management. On one of my early 'journeys to the moon' I discovered I was performing some dental procedures that could more cost effectively have been accomplished by a registered dental assistant whose salary is approximately two percent of the amount an efficient dentist charges per hour. I saw the dramatic impact effective delegation of specific portions of procedures can have on the bottom line. Whenever a less costly (in terms of salary, wages, or payroll) teammate is able to perform a duty as well or better than the one currently performing the task, it is more efficient and cost effective to reassign the task. This freed up some time for me, and was key to moving the organization in a favorable direction.

All businesses are either growing or they are not. If they are not, they are likely being passed up by the competition. Therefore, the business that has reached a plateau is not necessarily stable, but is often declining relative to other enterprises in its field.

For the successful business, growth must be a constant and unceasing goal. Since growth is so important, let's take a look at strategies for growth.

STRATEGIES FOR GROWTH:

EXPAND THE MARKET

The small candle-making business, mentioned previously, origi-nally sold their product to tourists out of a small retail outlet in the building where they made the candles. The first clue that things were happening was when an employee mentioned the fact that they had a contract with the Dayton Hudson Company, a major retailer. Now hundreds of employees and several thousands of square feet of man-ufacturing plant later, they are shipping candles around the world on a daily basis. In this instance the market was expanded from over-the-counter sales at the manufacturing plant to contracts with major retailers and on to global expansion.

Expanding the market may also mean educating existing cus-tomers for greater utility of your existing product or service. Let's say you have a house cleaning service and have eight regular cus-tomers that you serve weekly. You might suggest spring-cleaning gift certificates for your regular customers or holiday cleaning for their relatives and friends. This not only increases revenue for the present, but also introduces your fine service to many other potential customers.

PUBLICITY

Publicity is wonderful and one of the reasons is that by definition it is free. Publicity is communication that is transmitted through a mass media at no charge. There are several types and nearly endless ways of tapping this important vein that can promote success.

— News releases- usually fewer than 300 words

— Feature articles- longer than news release

— Captioned photograph- explains photograph

— Press conference- to announce major news event

Like my good friend and partner Dr. Herman Boehme says, "Every newspaper editor sits down with a blank piece of paper in front of him every morning. If you have an interesting story to tell, you are his friend!"

Your creativity, charisma, humor, and ability to show your business in its best light can often bring you public exposure that is far more valuable than any advertising you could even dream of affording. If you are able to get your business or yourself in the press (in a positive way), in the news section or public interest section of a local publication, your story will be widely read. Were you to spend massive funds on advertising, your customers and potential customers often have what seems to be an 'unconscious radar' which guides them right on by most advertisements.

When someone gets involved in a special interest story they are introduced to you and/or your business indirectly. This indirect method of learning of a business often stimulates curiosity that may lead to their becoming a customer. Research shows the subtle approach to be much more effective than attempting to 'hit the customer over the head and drag them in'.

The creative mind is able to come up with many publicity applications. For instance, one of my early business ventures was a recreational fishing business. We found that newspapers were more than willing to print pictures of local children with large fish. The fact that our identifying company logo was always prominently displayed in the "fish picture" was no deterrent to publication. The headline on the sports page, or even the front page, "Local Girl Lands Trophy Fish" or "Local Boy with His Limit of Walleyes" greatly promoted our business.

Another example of publicity: in my youth our family tapped maple trees in the spring of the year and made maple syrup which was sold to tourists during the summer season. Newspaper editors would love to come to our "sugar bush" and do feature articles of the "Maple Syrup Production Process." It made for a woodsy, homey, pioneering feature article that had high reader appeal. Unfortunately, (or on the other hand maybe it should be looked at as fortunate as it surely did head me in another direction) the maple syrup business was so extremely labor intensive for the money received that it was a poor way to make a living. Finding the right livelihood seems often a process of eliminating a lot of 'good ways not to make a living along the way'. This maple syrup operation was in northern Minnesota. Years later I discovered the northeastern states, like Maine and Vermont, typically get maple syrup harvests three to four times as generous per tree tapped as we received for the same effort. This apparently is due to climactic variations. This is a great example of being in the wrong place at the right time. The maple syrup business can, in retrospect, be viewed as a great opportunity for learning. On the plus side it left wonderful memories of being close to nature in the woods in the spring, and a good baseline from which to recognize other opportunities with more profit potential.

Your ability to take advantage of publicity to leverage your business is limited only by your imagination. Give your wonderful, creative imagination full reign and discover how you might benefit from your own unique situation.

Generally, small weekly publications are the most likely to be interested in your story. Once published there, it often attracts the attention of larger publications. You may find it awkward to bring the weekly article to the attention of the larger daily newspapers, however a friend or agent can do it easily. Also, by befriending the first publishing editor you may be able to encourage him to pass the article on to a friend or peer in a larger newspaper.

If you enjoy writing, periodically submit a story of interest to local newspapers. This keeps the public aware of you and informed about developments in your field. There are many routes to attaining publicity for your business, whatever it is.

One good way to become known in your community is to consider speaking engagements. Although most people are reluctant to speak in front of a group, or worse, a TV camera, there is an avenue to assist you. Join a local chapter of the Toastmaster's International which typically have weekly meetings and before you know it, you will love to speak in front of a group. Many local organizations are actively seeking speakers. Talk show hosts are interested in local success stories. The publicity you would receive from such engagements is well worth the little effort expended.

EXTEND YOUR HOURS

For the service-oriented business, extended hours of operation can greatly increase profits. We are a service thirsty culture who tends to flock toward the competitor who is most sensitive to our needs, desires, or whims. When an entrepreneur is successful at catering to one or even all three of the above he has found the winning combination. Customers are constantly voting, with their dollars, for the most successful business in a market. They want to spend these dollars at their own convenience, not at the business' convenience.

A friend of ours owned a custom-designed jewelry store in an exclusive resort area in a desert urban setting. It was located in a two-story mall right at the entrance, with windows facing the street. The mall hours were from 10 am to 9 pm as posted, and most merchants arrived reluctantly a few minutes before 10 am. Our friend had noticed that many visitors in the resort area walked in the cooler morning hours (especially those attending conventions walked before their activities began). Thereafter, he opened his store at 8:30 am and did more business from 8:30 am to 10 am than all the other hours combined. The well-to-do convention attendees were grateful to find a store open and took advantage to do their gift shopping at their leisure in the early morning.

Extended hours for the service or retail business are often more profitable per hour than standard base hours for at least a couple of reasons. One, the fixed costs that are customarily considerable are already paid during the regular hours. You usually don't pay any more rent, real-estate taxes, or liability insurance when you extend your hours of service. As fixed costs remain constant, only variable costs, which are considerably less, are incurred during extended

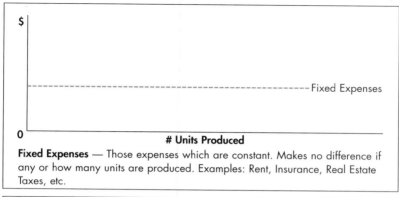

Fixed Expenses

Fixed Expenses — Those expenses which are constant. Makes no difference if any or how many units are produced. Examples: Rent, Insurance, Real Estate Taxes, etc.

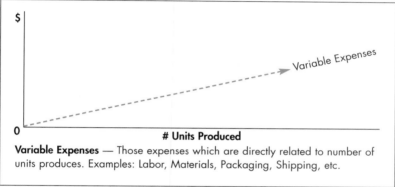

Variable Expenses

Variable Expenses — Those expenses which are directly related to number of units produces. Examples: Labor, Materials, Packaging, Shipping, etc.

Figure 16-1

hours. Therefore sales minus variable costs equals substantially higher profits. See figure 16-3

For the production type of business, similar economies with regard to fixed costs apply. The rent, machinery, insurance, taxes, etc. are already paid in order to operate the base hours. Therefore the marginal cost of each additional unit produced is now equal to the variable costs per unit of increased production. This variable cost per unit from extended hours of production often is only a small fraction of the cost per unit incurred during regular hours of production. See figure 16-2.

This reduced production cost of each additional unit produced

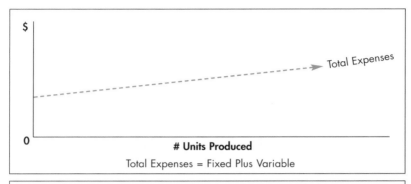

Total Expenses = Fixed Plus Variable

Income From Sales

Figure 16-2

may allow flexibility for significant discounts on volume orders. Or it may afford increased profits if a discount is not necessary. Add to this, economies of scale such as quantity purchasing, more efficient mass-production equipment and machinery that increased production numbers would justify, and you get a glimpse of how growth of your business may lead to substantial profits.

BROADEN YOUR PRODUCT OR SERVICE BASE

Once you have established customers, consider broadening the product line or services you are providing. This can often be accomplished at very little marginal cost per unit.

For instance, the minimal cost of offering scented candles to your current customers who are purchasing unscented candles is

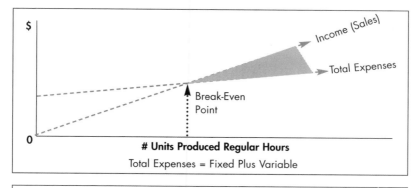

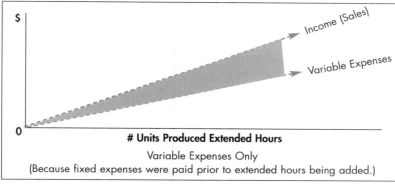

Figure 16-3 Note shaded area represents profit

small as you already have the molds, the wicks, a warehouse full of wax, and ship to the customers regularly. The payroll, utilities, an accountant and the rent have been paid. Liability insurance and the other necessities are in place. Therefore, you are likely to double your sales and increase your expenses, by only a small amount. Depending on your overhead this could easily quadruple profits, or much more. See figure 16.3

Note the more massive shaded 'profit area' in the extended hours graph.

NEW USES FOR EXISTING PRODUCTS

Prepare an "Emergency Survival Kit" with big, long-lasting candles and simple dishes to mount them on. Include a small box of matches with your company name, phone number, e-mail and ordering information printed on it. Put a sign at your cash register saying; "Don't let the California blackout get the best of your friends. Be prepared. Emergency Survival Kits for all power outages now on sale." You get the idea — build on something everyone is aware of.

A classic example from the past is baking soda — not to bake a cake but to use in the refrigerator for its deodorizing impact. How many refrigerators do you expect there are in the United States? In the world? How often should a new box of baking soda be purchased to replace the old box? Wow! Someone was thinking again!

GROWTH VIA ACQUISITION

Expansion through the acquisition of other businesses can be a legitimate strategy for growth of your existing business. Full and careful analysis is indicated prior to jumping into an additional business. Questions to ask might include:

— What if any connection is there, or could there be between my current business and the target business?

— Are the businesses complimentary?

— Are the businesses competitive?

— Are the businesses end users the same? similar? different?

— Might the products or services be bundled to promote sales?

— Why is the target business for sale?

— What profits might I expect to generate from the target business?

— Would it likely increase or decrease profits of my primary business?

— Would it make my life more or less enjoyable?

— Would it require too much of my time to manage?

Only when the positives far outweigh the negatives is one justified in pursuing the acquisition.

REPEAT CUSTOMERS

The impact of repeat business will depend to a large extent on the nature of your business. For most businesses it is important that once you have a happy customer, you retain that customer for the life of your business.

Some of the toughest, most cantankerous, sarcastic customers on initial contact have proven to be the very best business promoters once you win them over. This is often not too difficult to understand when you see it from the lunar perspective. These people go around all day long stimulating the worst in others with their sarcasm and unpleasant comments. When someone treats them with compassion, they are overwhelmed and tend to bond very readily. Once bonded with you and your business there is no end to what they will do to promote your business.

How do I retain that customer? Do whatever it takes to assure your customer is well pleased with your product or service. There are millions of repeat customers who will go farther, pay more, and in other ways put themselves out to do business with a particular individual or business whom they feel has treated them well. We will explore three of the many strategies for stimulating repeat customers: 'product', 'service', and 'bonding'.

PRODUCT

Depending on your business, product is at times the most difficult way to differentiate yourself from the competition. If you are in the grocery business, for instance, it is very difficult for you to convince your customers that your Cheerios are better than your competitors. However, if your business is built on a unique new product and you hold the patent, product can be your best ally. In this case, seriously review the section on *publicity*, as the media is often eager for new product stories, especially if you can add a little zest to the story through your creativity and imagination.

If your business falls between these two extremes (as most do), keep in mind that product difference, whether real or perceived, may be key to customer retention.

SERVICE

Service is of utmost importance in our society. Swift, friendly, respectful, courteous service is most often rewarded with high percentage repeat business. Customers are often willing to patronize your business once, and depending on their initial experience, they may repeat again if they are pleased, or never again, if the experience is negative. There is an old saying that "you only get one chance at a first impression". Do everything possible to make it a dynamite experience for your customers.

Companies with mottoes that all team members buy in to, such as "whatever it takes" or "service with a smile", and where we regularly hear "my pleasure," "of course," "no problem," "I'd be glad to" and the like are the ones with high numbers of repeat customers. When the customer gets what she wants, when she wants it and leaves with a smile on her face, she is more likely to return soon.

Service means many different things to different people. Following is a checklist to consider:

CONVENIENT HOURS

Few businesses get by with the traditional 9 am to 5 pm, five days a week, and the number is sure to further decrease in the future. Since a high percentage of your customers themselves likely work 9 to 5, they are not readily available to frequent your business during these hours.

More and more businesses are opening seven days per week. Also more 24-hour per day businesses are prospering. The additional cost for the extended open hours is typically minimal, consisting largely of increased payroll with possibly a slight utility increase. Take for instance the retailing giant Wal-Mart. If they were initially open 12 hours per day, their fixed costs, building, insurance, maintenance, etc., were already paid. When they choose to stay open 24 hours, their marginal cost per additional hour of keeping the store open is limited to a few hosts (as they like to call them), checkout personnel, and a little electricity.

VARIETY OF PRODUCTS OR SERVICES AVAILABLE

All other factors held constant, the more full service the business, the more successful tends to be the rule. Service is convenience. Customers prefer to make one stop and purchase all needed items, rather than to make several stops, and hunt for their car in the parking lots each time after shopping.

For example, a beauty salon was traditionally a place where women went to get a haircut or a permanent. Currently an advertisement in the yellow pages states, "hair, nails, tanning, massage, and now new body sugaring." Whatever body sugaring is! The point being, the wider the variety of related goods and/or services available, all other factors being equal, usually the more cost effectively they can be delivered. Also multiple related services at a single location is more convenient for the consumer. A good fit on both ends.

Even a specialty shop like the 'Body Shop', while limiting its products to a narrow range, offers a wide variety of oils, soaps, lotions, creams, and fragrances, so that one might expect to find nearly unlimited choices of related products at one location.

CONVENIENT ACCESS

In these days of more traffic and less parking spaces, convenient access is becoming more and more important. Therefore, the business that offers convenient access, ample free parking, drive-through service, and any other 'perks' for their customers has a leg up on the competition.

QUICK SERVICE

Little or no standing in line or waiting is directly related to customer satisfaction. As our lifestyles become busier, the value placed on our time is of increasing importance.

When evaluating prompt service, it is important that our perspective be from the vantage point of the customer, whose time is important. Therefore, location convenience is becoming an added value for your consideration.

Careful planning, preparation, and training of all team members can promote prompt friendly service delivered for maximum benefit to customer and business.

Customers remember the business they can walk into, perform their function, and get out all in one breath. Anything we can do to facilitate that happening will be rewarded.

FRIENDLY SERVICE

A friendly, welcoming smile as your customer enters your business will create a warm fuzzy feeling which can go a long way toward that pleasant experience you would like to create. Pleasantries such as please, thank you, good to see you again, thanks for your business, as well as addressing the customer by their name when possible are all adjuncts to success. Helpful service like explaining the differences between products or services and showing customers to a product, instead of pointing in a vague direction, all compound to equate business success. All people representing your business to the public must be courteous and friendly toward all customers at all times and at all costs. No exceptions.

BONDING

The 'knack' for developing a sense of closeness or compatibility with customers during the initial contact pays huge dividends for those willing to put forth the required effort to excel at this talent. A key to bonding is to understand that people tend to like people who are like themselves, or who have common interests or value systems, or in some other way possess a trait the customer can relate to. What does this all mean? It means that careful observation of your customer's slightest nuance can lead you to clues as to where he is coming from psychologically. For instance, you can learn a good deal just by the way your customer approaches you. When your customer approaches with a crisp gait and asks sternly, "Where's the service around here?," you would be advised to crisply respond, "You've come to the right place, sir. What might I do for you?" His subconscious mind tells him, "He's just like me! I've met someone just like me!" On the other hand, when your customer approaches hesitantly and softly inquires, "If it might be possible to look at one of your products", you quietly and slowly ask, "Which products might be of interest to you?"

The concept we are talking about here is what is called matching. At this point we need to make a distinction between matching and mimicking. Matching is to approximate the attitude, the demeanor, the general air of the customer. The intention is to be similar to but not attempt to duplicate the specifics of the customer. The subtle difference is that mimicking will surely irritate the customer, while the much less obvious matching tends to create a bonding phenomenon.

It is important to note that many cultures have distinct traits. For example, certain cultures like to bargain and are much more comfortable when they feel they have negotiated a deal. However, within each culture, individuals vary just as they do within your own. Once you have mastered the art of 'matching' with a certain culture you are often able to understand and react favorably to others of the same ethnic group. You could find yourself successfully profiting in a market segment of the population that has been largely neglected because no one has taken the time or effort to learn how to connect with this group.

ATTRIBUTES TO WATCH FOR AS OPPORTUNITIES TO BOND WITH YOUR CUSTOMERS:

EYE CONTACT

Some customers will approach and talk to you but never make eye contact. If they continually look down, do not stare at them, but focus your eyes on your shoes while carrying on your conversation. If this is a trait of their culture and not one of your culture, it does not make it wrong, it just makes it different from yours. Accept it and your customer will appreciate your response. Other customers may glance at your eyes and then quickly look away. Be alert to this trait and follow the approximate pattern established. Still other customers will give you the impression you are in a staring match. Attempt to win the stare-down; they will love it.

PROXIMITY

Potential customers have a certain range of distance from you that is most comfortable for them. Some aggressive males may want to be right in your face. This is most difficult for those who prefer let's say a three-foot separation for comfort. The aggressive customer often has the three-foot comfort zone clerk backing around the room attempting to gain a comfortable distance to no avail. The customer just keeps coming closer and no one is comfortable. The aggressor can't get close enough, and the three-foot away comfort zone clerk can't get far enough away. When it's the potential customer who desires the close range communication, the best option is to stand your ground and let him be in your face. After all, you are there to help your customer feel comfortable in your place of business, and actually no matter what you do he will be closer than you prefer so your best answer is to hold your position and accommodate your guest. On the other hand, when your customer's comfort distance is obviously greater than yours is, respect that desire and do not attempt to close the gap.

VOLUME

Some customers will talk very loudly. This may be a person who is hard of hearing or it may be a cultural trait, or an individual characteristic. Whatever the cause, your best response is to approximate the volume and tone, as this will tend to put them most at ease and more likely into the purchasing mode. With a soft-spoken customer, speak softly also.

SPEED

Be aware of the rapidity of speech and attempt to respond similarly. For some, speed is more of a challenge, but can surely be approximated with practice.

TEMPO

Some people tend to pause periodically...a sort of...time.... when they are...thinking about which word to select .....next. Be careful not to get caught mimicking. It probably is safest to just talk slowly and not try to approximate the pauses.

TONE

Tone of voice varies greatly and is very important to approach when possible. Watch the very extremes and just move toward them a notch or two from your normal voice and don't completely distort your voice in the process. Some people find it very easy to adjust tones, others do not. Practicing at tone sensitivity will pay off on the bottom line.

FACIAL EXPRESSIONS

Facial expressions vary all over the place. The subtlety in facial nuance is most revealing and interesting. This ranges all the way from very serious and concerned to sometimes playful and mischievous. Coming back with a response that is similar positively alters your customer's entire outlook on the potential transaction.

GRAMMAR

Careful observation of grammar and word usage are often very useful in the building of rapport, as well as being key to understanding your customer. When a customer communicates in a very smooth and polished manner we could guess he is probably accustomed to some of the finer luxuries in life and is likely to be appreciative of fine quality. Toward the opposite end of the spectrum we might suspect that his interests might well lean toward value and/or price factors. However, be careful not to prejudge your customer too quickly, as there are many exceptions to these generalities.

POSTURE

Posture also leaves clues. These range from depression to high self-esteem and all gradients in between. While we do not want to go to that depressing place, the closer you come to matching the other postures the greater the propensity for bonding. While this list is not exhaustive, it is a good start and by being aware, you can practice some of these techniques. When you do, you'll position yourself far ahead of the competition.

OTHER WAYS TO PROMOTE REPEAT CUSTOMERS

POLITENESS

Simple please, thank-you, appreciate your business, my pleasure, certainly, thanks for stopping in, have a great day, and any other positive appropriate comments go a long way toward your goal of a pleasant encounter.

ENTHUSIASM

Enthusiastic employees are a tremendous asset for your business. It is contagious and tends to stimulate brisk sales. Paying top dollar for customer contact teammates is one of the best investments you can make to ensure your success.

APPEARANCE

Crisp, clean, snappy, uniformed when appropriate, team members contribute to the image of a successful business. Uniforms lead to an air of organization, confidence, and uniformity and also make it convenient for your customers to recognize who is available to assist them. Uniforms are also most beneficial in promoting dress codes, which may otherwise be difficult to manage.

PERSONALITY

An associate with an outgoing, accommodating, smiling personality to greet your customers as they approach or phone your business does not cost, it pays. Like one sign in an employee lounge reads, "Get Happy or Get Out."

KNOWLEDGEABLE

Well-trained and knowledgeable people representing your business are mandatory. The more help you are able to provide for your customers, the more brisk will be your sales. Effort spent training enthusiastic team members to better serve customers pays large dividends in return. For example, many observers were quite surprised to see Home Depot hire licensed electricians to serve customers in their electrical department, licensed plumbers to answer questions for their amateur plumbing customers in the plumbing department, professional painters in their paint department, and so forth. Look at the record — Home Depot's success and growth speaks for itself. The more you can be of service to your customers, the more they vote for you with their business dollars. It is impossible in the long term to give more to your customers than you receive in return.

FIRST IMPRESSION

You never get a second chance at a first impression. Therefore, make certain your first impression is so favorable you don't need a second chance. By the time a new customer has had four seconds of exposure to your business, an impression has been formed. If it is negative, you may never change it. Therefore, it is of supreme importance to concentrate sufficient effort to planning that these first four seconds are positive.

To make sure of this happening, we must look at what the customer sees, hears, feels, smells, and what they may sense. Let's discuss how we might stack the deck in our favor in each of these categories.

Visual input is undoubtedly the first consideration, for the majority of people are strongly impressed by what they see the moment they enter a business for the first time. Aspects of what they see can be grouped into the following: color, texture, light, and arrangement of the room.

Color is very important. If you want to create a warm, welcome environment, choose from the earth tones or muted earth tones. If a clean and or sterile impression is appropriate, then pure whites may be indicated. When a light-hearted, fun-loving impression is desired, light pinks, yellows, and blues will help. For drama, highly contrasting, bold colors make a definite statement.

Texture, while more subtle than color, has considerable impact on the first impression. Rough surfaces such as brick, rough-surfaced lumber and coarsely-textured walls might be magnificent for your mountain climbing accessory store, but totally inappropriate for a fine china shop. In some settings a slight to modest contrast in texture can be most appealing to the eye.

Light is a huge factor in creating atmosphere. In discussing light, we must consider natural light and artificial light. For daytime hours in your place of business, natural light, when it can be taken advantage of, is very helpful in creating a favorable ambiance. For dark days, pre-sunrise and post-sunset hours, artificial lighting can do much for your desired effect. Indirect lighting on dimmers might offer moods from calm to romantic. Use spot lights and flood lights for drama, and high intensity lights for drawing attention to a particular product or display.

ROOM APPEARANCE

Depending upon the business, a neat and tidy entrance with an open aspect tends to be inviting. This is in stark contrast to the cluttered, haphazard, magazine-strewn room we have all seen far too often.

Sound of gentle, upbeat background music has been found to

increase spending, whereas too loud, too harsh sounds can drive customers off. Background music will soften the hum of the high speed turbine in a dental office. The "idle teammate" noises, where associates bunch together and talk and laugh, is wise to eliminate in the successful business. Other inherent sounds such as machine shop noises or restaurant kitchen noises of dishes clattering and the like tend to be distractive and best muffled out with background sounds.

Odors may be offensive or compelling, so be strictly aware of any and all odors. An example might be the restaurant or bakery who vents the kitchen exhaust fan out onto the sidewalk, to let the tantalizing aromas entice the customers. In contrast is the musty, stale odor in some shops which make you want to leave the moment you open the front door.

Experiencing the feeling one gets when entering your place of business is a culmination of all of the above and more. One of the most important factors is a pleasant smile and a cheery greeting from a well-groomed, neat store attendant. This quick, spontaneous, caring attention often clinches the favorable first impression. What they think and what they sense is directly related to what they feel. Good feelings produce positive thoughts and you have a sense of accomplishment in having found this business.

What can be the result of the successful first transaction? Let's say you are in the grocery business, and your neighborhood potential customer shops once a week. In fifteen years we are looking at seven hundred and eighty transactions, all hinging on that first pleasant visit to your grocery store. If it is not a good first impression, chalk up seven hundred eighty transactions for your competitor.

In summary, the seemingly extreme effort put forth in setting the stage for "the first four seconds" in your place of business will surely pay back generous premiums for your effort. If your first four seconds are not able to favorably impress your potential customer, and you are not able to turn it around before she leaves, she will likely end up a customer of your competition.

GO THE EXTRA MILE

Whenever you are able to give more than is expected of you, your customers will be pleasantly surprised. As this quality becomes known in the community, your company will be recognized as one that goes the extra mile to please their customers and your business will grow proportionately.

There are many ways of giving more than is expected of you. An example, on the initial customer contact, if you can discern what the customer is expecting, you are one leg up on the competition. This important information can come from various sources, such as:

— Comments made on the phone prior to your first meeting.

— Discovering which one of your competitors your new customer did business with prior to choosing you and knowing what their "modus operandi" is.

— By being familiar with what the industry standards are you will be in a better position to determine what customers are likely to expect.

— Asking the new customer about their special requirement. They will often let you know. For example, if they request that their orders be shipped within three working days, tell them you are shipping within 24 hours, and do it.

DISCOVERING YOUR CUSTOMERS' 'HOT BUTTON'

Most everyone has different priorities and a different value system. The importance of satisfying your customer's highest priorities

217

cannot be overstressed. Sounds great you say, "but how can I possibly get into my customers' minds to find the order of their priorities?" Well, you do not need to get into their mind. Be alert to nuances and remarks. Ask a lot of questions, like, what is most important to you in this widget? Is consistency of size more important than color? Is length more important than weight? Is price more important than delivery time? Is design more important than function? And the list goes on.

It sounds like a lot of effort, and at times it surely is. However, sometimes your customers may come right out and tell you exactly what they want. The key is to listen and watch expressions and body language closely as the person is communicating. By carefully observing and getting a good feel for where they are headed, then asking key questions, one often obtains information quickly. Once you discover your customer's 'hot button' you have important information. Act on it.

When you have gained a feel for your customer's priorities, it is up to you to cater to them. For instance, if quick service is the highest priority of the community, provide quick, friendly service and enjoy success. On the other hand, if your customer needs precision, say your component is part of a very expensive machine and they require your tolerance to be plus or minus .001 inch. Design your production and quality control to a tolerance of only .0005 inch and they will be thrilled with your precision. Whatever they want, strive to give them more than they thought was possible.

Whatever your business, there is some aspect of it where you can serve your community better in the future than they have been served. The one who steps out in front and offers the superior service is the one who is most often rewarded handsomely.

ATTITUDE OF DOING MORE THAN EXPECTED

Individuals that are financially successful across the board tend to do more than expected in all dealings, not just business-related events. This suggests that this tendency is not just surface behavior. Those persons who consistently 'go the extra mile' are, in a sense, prepaying insurance against failure. This trait is so refreshing and so very much appreciated that not only do the beneficiaries of this treatment return for more of the same, but they also tell a large number of their friends, relatives, and associates about their experience. This will result in stimulating even more enthusiasm for your products or services.

As customers become accustomed to a higher level of service provided, the 'extra milers' seem to find a continuous string of new surprises to keep their customers pleased. These innovators tend to set a higher standard and then raise the bar again and again. This is why they are the winners, and climb the success ladder most rapidly. They are driven by the satisfaction of a job well done. The side effect is that the happy recipients continue to promote their businesses for them.

It is impossible to 'out give' your customers in the long term. The more you give to your customers, the more your customers give back in return. Your extra effort, when given unselfishly and without direct intent of reciprocation, often yields a return far beyond what your wildest imagination could have envisioned.

17

DO WHAT YOU LOVE

*"Man is not the creature of circumstances.
Circumstances are the creatures of men."*
                                        Disraeli

THE VAST MAJORITY of millionaires studied loved what they were doing. So much so that they often worked 12 or 16 hours a day and regretted that they were too tired to continue. What a contrast to the classic clock-watchers we are all familiar with.

The entrepreneur who is engrossed in a productive activity most assuredly will contribute more to society than a person who is just doing his job. The fortunate one who 'loses himself' in his work not only works longer hours, but is likely more productive each hour. Gratification from his efforts motivates him to higher and higher levels. He finds himself on a wonderful upward spiral that is self-perpetuating.

How does one get into this situation?

One approach is to first find something you love doing. We are all born with different talents, abilities, and tendencies that predispose us to like, or dislike various occupations we brush up against in the course of our development. Never linger in a situation just because it pays more, sounded good at the time but turned out to be a dead-end, or was simply available at the time you needed a job.

As an example, we know a young man who fell into the job of taxicab dispatcher. He loved his work and as time went on, rose to chief dispatcher with a commensurate salary.

The only problem — he had always disliked the city where he worked. Unfortunately, a thorough knowledge of streets and businesses, acquired over a long period of time, was necessary for his high-paying position. He had made the error of not planning ahead and finding a more compatible area before it was too late.

A second approach might be to find a profitable business and if necessary, redesign the daily activities to your liking, building on its previous success. In this case be careful not to make major changes which might have a negative impact on a flourishing business. Do not change things that were previously accepted in the community. The business success is the reason you bought the business in the first place. If at the end of an evaluation period you have analyzed the possibility of changes (different hours, etc.), slowly implement them and observe the response.

Watch yourself for peak experiences. When do these occur? Was it when you were alone? Was it in a group setting? Maybe that's a clue. Perhaps you function best in the group environment. What types of people do you interact with best? Is it the methodical analytical type, or is spontaneity important to you?

You'll want an environment that is not irritating. Avoid a sawmill if you can't stand loud noise. This seems almost too elementary to mention, but it is unbelievable how many people end up spending their working lives in their worst possible environments.

One thing we have learned from successful entrepreneurs is that they have often done many different things before they found their calling. This breed is not hesitant to try something new. If it doesn't work out, they try another avenue. Some, of course, have known at an early age exactly what they want to do. These succeeders also have the habit of picturing themselves in other people's occupations when the opportunity arises. They are able to evaluate the positives and negatives and usually conclude they are most suited for their current position.

The fairy tale version, which may happen occasionally, is about the lucky lassie who does what she loves, throws herself into it and tons of money falls from the skies all around her. Unfortunately this usually is not the case. Difficult as discovering what you love to do may seem, it is often considered the easy part. Reaping substantial rewards for your efforts is usually the real challenge.

Doing whatever you do just a little better can tip the balance and cause a landslide victory for your business. It is often a close call, for a large number of potential customers, whether they choose product A or B, or whether they visit X or Z for their services. Any slight edge can turn the tide. Malcolm Gladwell, Little Brown and Co. dramatically illustrates this fact in *The Tipping Point*, copyright 2000. He explains in detail how little things can make a real difference. A worthwhile book.

Constantly look for opportunities that will give you a competitive advantage, and capitalize on them. This brings to mind the super star baseball player whose batting average is only a few percentage points higher than his teammates, yet he earns ten or twenty times their salary.

Here are a few examples to stimulate your thinking about your own business:

PACKAGING

This could mean a customer friendly package, as opposed to the current bubble pack that takes the great Hercules with a butcher knife to open. It could also mean simply combining services like a hair cut with a permanent wave and offering a special discount for the combination.

SYSTEMS

Your advantage might come from the systems you implement. For example, an effective telephone system whereby telephones are answered pleasantly and promptly may make just that small difference between you and your competitors.

FREE GIFTS

Free gifts for visiting your retail outlet or inquiring about your service can be effective far beyond their cost, especially when gifts can be purchased in large volume at a steep discount. Sometimes a supplier of gifts may recognize the benefit of your promoting his product as your gift and afford you an additional discount, but 'if you don't ask, you don't get.' This is an important rule to keep in mind always.

DISCOUNTS

Customers love discounts! So much so it might even be considered a suitable spectator sport to visit some of these giant department store promotions where people line up for blocks to get in for 70% or 80% discounts on a limited supply of goods. You may witness customers push and shove and grab for merchandise and at times almost come to 'fisticuffs' over certain items. These sales are typically quite successful, not directly because of the sales of merchandise at a heavy discount, but because by getting masses of customers into the store, much merchandise not on sale is also purchased. The latter category, the full price goods, is where the majority of the profit is made.

The astute spectator observes how the buying frenzy environment created by the shrewd marketers is contagious to the degree that once the sale items are depleted, much appetite for merchandise remains. What a nice convenience to have all these frenzied customers in your store with all your tempting items at this point in their emotional cycle.

In summary, every business is unique to some extent and therefore offers its own opportunities for the creative manager to differentiate his product or service from his competitors. The more successful she is at being the one that stands out in a positive way, the more prosperous she becomes. Large to huge profits are possible to those of you who have made the extra effort to build or purchase their own businesses. These profits, however, are not available simply because you own your own business, but must be earned by the votes of the community you are serving. These votes come in the form of dollars spent for your products and/or services. The more you please those enthusiastic customers which comprise your community, the more votes you receive. In business, unlike some recent elections, all other factors held constant, the business receiving the most votes wins. Here is wishing you the very best and most prosperous business journey. You deserve it.

18

FOR THE BOSS ONLY

"The way of superior man is threefold;
virtuous, he is free from anxieties;
wise, he is free from perplexities;
bold, he is free from fear."

Confucius

NOW AS YOU are in charge of your own business, you may find it often is quite lonely. Even with the greatest team, you still have to make the decisions and are solely responsible. The wise entrepreneur looks for a trusted individual, let's call him a Mentor, to consult with frequently. This Mentor should be a person not involved in your business and completely unbiased in their approach to comments about your business.

There are expensive consultants available who will examine your affairs and give you their advice on how to solve existing problems. They will give you a detailed write-up and a bill for their service, then most often walk away. What you need is someone who is available to help you see clearly what course of action would be best in difficult situations. This person is someone that is on your side, to point out alternatives and let you make the decisions. There will be times you just need someone who cares enough about you to really listen and not criticize. Respect his thoughts and appreciate his kindness.

One excellent free resource is the U.S. Small Business Administration's SCORE program. The Service Core of Retired Executives has chapters all over the nation and their service is free; just call for an appointment.

Your greatest assets will be your teammates. The way you treat them will be a big part of your success. Make them all members of your team, call them associates or team members rather than employees. Have regular staff meetings, and, if you are a small group, take them out for breakfast. With a larger group, meet separately with each department. This is a time not to pontificate but to listen to your people, encouraging them to participate and voice new business ideas. Remember that they are often closer to the customers on a daily basis than you are. Write down any suggestions and evaluate them carefully. It is important that you report back if you use their new idea. Make everyone a partner. Don't hesitate to tell them when things are not going well and seek their help. You are all involved together for a common good.

Have a profit-sharing plan in place; this will do wonders for the attitude of your team. A real benefit for you will result as they police themselves and weed out the non-producers. When it happens that you have to terminate an employee, try to help them find a job they are better fitted for and you will still be their friend.

Even a very small organization can have a health insurance plan for all people on the team. Often trade associations will sponsor this kind of coverage at affordable costs.

Hire only the best people you can find, and don't hesitate if they know more than you do in a particular area of your business. Learn from them, but do not forget you have the last word on any decision. Also, tap the teenagers who are looking to be trainees through high school programs. If no specific programs are available, contact the high school and ask about students looking for after school, weekend, or summer positions. At times, one phone call has yielded 15 or 20 interviews. We have been very pleased with the bright, enthusiastic young recruits local high schools have sent us. Also many have stayed part-time on through their college years. We have even experienced some of these young recruits become full-time teammates after graduating from college. It is a most rewarding and heart-warming experience to watch these people mature in the business environment.

Once a year, plan on a retreat with your senior people. It doesn't have to be a fancy place, but a day or two away from the office. Planning sessions like this can be very productive and you have a chance to see how people interact with each other. This often provides great insight for future promotions.

Plan for an emergency (just your own plan), don't decimate your plan, it will only start rumors and anxieties. What would you do if you had a fire, a natural disaster, etc.? Be prepared to act decisively and hope you will never need to implement the plan.

Participate in trade shows both as an exhibitor and a customer; you will likely meet more people involved in your line of work in a few days than in any other place. You can see what your competition is up to and make some meaningful business connections.

A last, but not least, suggestion is to go out and meet your customers personally. If you have a sales force, go with each salesman on his calls. Listen to what the customer has to say — why are they buying or not buying. Be a hero and close the sale for one of your people who has been trying to close for some time. It will pay off in a big way. Most of all, have fun and give the person you are helping all of the credit.

SUMMARY — REALIZING YOUR FINANCIAL GOALS

"The thing about these critical success factors is that they are incredibly common things. What we determined is that if we could do these common things uncommonly well, we could be very successful."

Kevin Campbell

ISN'T IT EXCITING to know your financial goals are within your reach? Financial success may take more effort than some are willing to put forth. This allows those of us who have the burning desire to succeed to be able to separate ourselves from the rest of the pack.

We have discussed many of the principles followed by the successful wealth accumulators. By learning the basics from them and following their lead, we are definitely headed in the right direction for the attainment of our financial goals. In addition, we have explained many strategies and philosophies that will be beneficial to you in your endeavor to succeed.

Many people contend that 'luck' plays a big role in financial success. Careful observation confirms that the vast majority of luck occurs when preparedness meets opportunity. Opportunities are something we all brush up against from time to time. Preparedness is an element over which each individual is responsible. The well-prepared person will be in a much better position to capitalize on opportunities. For instance, we observed earlier that 80% of the first generation millionaires have at least a college education and many have advanced degrees. If you desire to climb the corporate ladder by joining one of the many great corporations in this country, a college education is absolutely necessary. If you are going into your own business, it is very important that you are well versed in the field that you enter. As we previously pointed out, you need a working knowledge of accounting, in particular, cost accounting, and an understanding of your financial statements.

Sorry, but any excuses about not having financial or emotional support for a college education does not cut much slack from those of us who have totally financed our college education on our own by working a number of jobs simultaneously, while attending college. Age is not an excuse either. It's never too late to attend the college of your choice.

Twenty percent of the first generation millionaires did not have a college education. These folks just had the 'whatever it takes' attitude and took advantage of opportunities as they were presented. Some of these successful people are well aware that it is possible to be well educated without subjecting oneself to the rigors of a formal education.

Many trades accept apprentice positions where it is possible for the determined, conscientious individual to learn the trade. A trade can lead to starting or purchasing a business that will be a vehicle to financial independence. If one of the trades appeal to you, go for it. Also many opportunities are available where the ambitious person can start at the bottom and work themselves up the ladder of success without a formal education.

In summary, we have covered many approaches for accomplishing your financial goals. Our list is by no means exhaustive, but affords some examples that might serve to stimulate the creative juices for the idea that strikes a cord for you. As the great late Napoleon Hill taught us in his classic Think And Grow Rich, which we highly recommend, "whatever your mind can conceive and believe, you can achieve".

Each individual is unique. It's entirely possible we have not hit on your exact solution, but hopefully have stimulated your thinking. All of us who are willing to put forth the required effort, eventually will discover what is right and natural for us. If you concentrate on finding a suitable business, it is simply a matter of time until the right opportunity comes along.

This is wonderful, because now that you know the basics, it's time to set your financial goals and create a plan for achieving them. It's important that you put your goals and your plan for attaining them in writing, then refer to them regularly. This will help you stay focused on your goals.

By using the following general principles laid out in prior chapters, and sticking with them, you will eventually find success on your side.

— Focus your available funds on appreciating assets.

— Get the forces of interest on your side, by drastically reducing interest paid out while increasing the interest you are receiving.

— Keep abreast of your financial statement so you are able to closely monitor your net worth.

— Constantly watch for ways to increase your assets and decrease your liabilities.

In time your financial discipline and efforts will result in the accumulation of a respectable nest egg. This achievement is significant as it serves as a motivating force for continued contributions and further growth. By developing a great appreciation of the forces of financial momentum and applying the principles learned, you are able to turn the financial tide in your favor.

When involved in a relationship where financial responsibilities are shared, you are aware that working together with respect to financial philosophies and goals is of utmost importance. As the row-boat metaphor illustrates when both mates are rowing with equal force, the rowboat glides smoothly to its desired destination. So likewise you are on a smooth journey to your financial goals when both partners are thinking and acting in a similar vein to achieve their mutual financial goals.

Realizing how rewarding it can be to live below your means, even as you observe others around you overspending their resources, is an important step toward riches. You know that spending more and more money on expendables and depreciating assets does not lead to increased happiness. The belief that increased spending will increase happiness is like a mirage in the distance, because once one gets close, it vanishes.

Your real leg up on your peers is your discipline to save regularly. This puts you in a small group headed for financial independence.

Carefully planning all purchases is beneficial, as it serves to protect you from impulse buying. Striving to get top value for all your purchases gives you a good feeling of accomplishment as well as conserving funds for financial growth.

Learning the 'moon perspective' technique is of great benefit. Regularly using this ability to view your challenges allows you the opportunity of solving most any dilemma by viewing it from a much broader and emotionally detached perspective.

Your venture into the world of business opens doors and opportunities. Owning your own business sets you free to work as long and hard as you see fit in order to attain your goals.

A significant discovery is realizing that better serving the community in your own unique way merits substantial financial rewards. The more creative you become in your efforts to serve others the more you earn.

Discovering the 'under promise over deliver' philosophy of life makes your daily journey significantly more pleasant as people are continually pleased and grateful. Happy customers are a reward in themselves and as a bonus they tend to promote your business, which has the potential for a substantial increase in profits.

Maximizing your rewards for doing what you love is the icing on the cake. When you are adding value to other people's lives, and loving the process, it is self-fulfilling and generally financially rewarding.

Reaching or exceeding your financial goals is the reward you deserve for the discipline and extra effort expended. This is the free enterprise system whereby compensation is intended to be commensurate with the magnitude of your contributions. Your success is proof the system is functioning properly.

Many thanks for taking this literary journey with us. Here's hoping you enjoyed it as much as we enjoyed preparing it for you. We will be looking forward to seeing you on top of the financial heap. Congratulations.

RECOMMENDED READING LIST

Think and Grow Rich by Napoleon Hill

The Tipping Point by Malcolm Gladwell

Mission Success by Og Mandino

The Greatest Salesman in the World by Og Mandino

Security Analysis by Ben Graham and David Dodd

The Millionaire Next Door by Stanley and Danko

Key to Yourself By Venice Bloodworth

The Millionaire by Wagner and Winnikoff

Psychocybernetics by Dr. Maxwell Maltz

Choices by Shad Helmsetter

Creative Mind by Earnest Holmes

The Lazy Man's Way to Riches by Joe Karbo

How to Better Yourself Through Mind Control by Burt Goldman

Warren Buffet, Master of the Market by Steele

Beating the Street by Peter Lynch

Winning on Wall Street by Martin Zweig

Cyber Investing by David I. Brown and Kassandra Bentley

Wall Street Words by David L. Scott

Super Stocks by Kenneth L. Fisher

100 Minds That Made the Market by Kenneth L. Fisher

The Wall Street Waltz by Kenneth L. Fisher

Buffetology by Mary Buffet

Unlimited Power by Anthony Robbins

INDEX

ORDER FORM

- Fax orders: 218-534-3949

- Telephone orders: Call toll free 1-800-450-0091
  (American Express, Visa or MasterCard)

- Postal Orders: Silk Pages Publishing
  21343 Archibald Road, P.O. Box 385
  Deerwood, MN 56444, USA

Please send the following:

Quantity:

_____ *How the Wealthy Get That Way* $17.95
     by Dr. Edward L. Silker

_____ *DENTISTRY: Building Your Million Dollar Solo Practice*.....$59.95
     by Dr. Edward L. Silker

_____ *DETAILS of the Million Dollar Practice*............................$59.95
     by Dr. Edward L. Silker

_____ Silker/Glickman Rubber Dam Clamps:
     1 Clamp.......................$15.00
     2-4 Clamps...........$13.00 each
     More than 4 ....$12.00 each

Sales Tax: MINNESOTA residents please add 6.5% sales tax.

Shipping and handling:
Surface Shipping: $2.00 (USA) for first book, $1.00 for each additional book (May take 3-4 weeks.)

Air Mail: $4.00 for first book, $2.00 for each additional book.

International orders please specify: ____ Air Mail ____ Surface

I wish to make payment by one of the following:

☐ Personal Check

☐ Credit Card: ___Visa ___MasterCard ___American Express

Card Number: _____

Name on Card: _____ Exp. Date: _____

Call TOLL FREE and order now!

ORDER FORM

- Fax orders: 218-534-3949

- Telephone orders: Call toll free 1-800-450-0091
  (American Express, Visa or MasterCard)

- Postal Orders: Silk Pages Publishing
  21343 Archibald Road, P.O. Box 385
  Deerwood, MN 56444, USA

Please send the following:

Quantity:

_____ *How the Wealthy Get That Way* $17.95
     by Dr. Edward L. Silker

_____ *DENTISTRY: Building Your Million Dollar Solo Practice*.....$59.95
     by Dr. Edward L. Silker

_____ *DETAILS of the Million Dollar Practice*..............................$59.95
     by Dr. Edward L. Silker

_____ Silker/Glickman Rubber Dam Clamps:
     1 Clamp........................$15.00
     2-4 Clamps...........$13.00 each
     More than 4 ....$12.00 each

Sales Tax: MINNESOTA residents please add 6.5% sales tax.

Shipping and handling:
Surface Shipping: $2.00 (USA) for first book, $1.00 for each additional book (May take 3-4 weeks.)
Air Mail: $4.00 for first book, $2.00 for each additional book.
International orders please specify: _____ Air Mail _____ Surface

I wish to make payment by one of the following:

☐ Personal Check

☐ Credit Card: ___Visa ___MasterCard ___American Express

Card Number: _____

Name on Card: _____ Exp. Date: _____

Call TOLL FREE and order now!